THE EMPTY PAY-CHECK

ALIGNING PURPOSE, INTENT, AND SUCCESS

AAKASH SINGH

BLUEROSE PUBLISHERS
India | U.K.

Copyright © Aakash Singh 2025

All rights reserved by author. No part of this publication may be reproduced, stored in a retrieval system or transmitted in any form or by any means, electronic, mechanical, photocopying, recording or otherwise, without the prior permission of the author. Although every precaution has been taken to verify the accuracy of the information contained herein, the publisher assumes no responsibility for any errors or omissions. No liability is assumed for damages that may result from the use of information contained within.

BlueRose Publishers takes no responsibility for any damages, losses, or liabilities that may arise from the use or misuse of the information, products, or services provided in this publication.

For permissions requests or inquiries regarding this publication, please contact:

BLUEROSE PUBLISHERS
www.BlueRoseONE.com
info@bluerosepublishers.com
+91 8882 898 898
+4407342408967

ISBN: 978-93-6783-588-3

Cover design: Daksh
Typesetting: Sagar

First Edition: January 2025

"Intentionality sharpens effort; purpose gives it wings"

To my family, friends, mentors, and to life itself—thank you for shaping me, challenging me, and believing in me, even when I didn't. Every lesson, every setback, and every moment of support made this journey possible.

Preface

The Real Cost of an Empty Paycheck

The year was 2011, and like the countless tides of young Indian students before me, I found myself walking into an engineering college. Automobile engineering, to be precise. The idea of studying cars and engines felt... exciting. I loved the sound of a roaring engine, the thrill of a winding road, the romance of speed. But loving cars as a "user" and devoting my life to understanding their every nut and bolt? Those were two entirely different things.

I didn't choose this path with intent. It wasn't a passion or a calling. My parents encouraged it softly, my older brother was already pursuing engineering, and nearly everyone in my circle was doing the same. In that world, engineering wasn't just a career choice, it was the default setting. It seemed safe, secure, and socially acceptable.

But the cracks in my decision began to show almost immediately. In my classes, I was surrounded by students who were fascinated by the intricacies of torque and combustion, while I sat quietly, disconnected from the enthusiasm around me. For me, it was just an endless cycle of lectures, assignments, and exams. I stumbled through, failing more tests than I'd care to admit, dragging myself across the finish line after four years. When the dust settled, my classmates had their sights set on master's degrees, specializations, and dream careers in the automotive industry. And me? I had no idea where to go next.

When you don't know where to go, you often end up walking away. That's exactly what I did. While my friends were busy planning their futures in engineering, I took a different path. I had been working part-time at a startup during my final year, and even though it had absolutely nothing to do with engineering, I decided to go all in.

This wasn't a decision born out of clarity or conviction. It was born out of desperation. I didn't know what I wanted, but I knew what I didn't want. I wanted nothing to do with engineering.

It wasn't long before the questions started rolling in. "Why would you throw away four years of hard work?" "What about your degree?" "You're making a mistake." I didn't have the answers then, but I pushed forward anyway.

The startup felt like freedom at first, but the novelty wore off quickly. I wasn't good at my job, and I certainly didn't love it. I was showing up every day for one reason: the pay check. That pay check kept the lights on, but it couldn't fill the growing void inside me. I woke up every morning with a heaviness in my chest, knowing I was stepping into another day of meaningless work. The days blurred together, each one heavier than the last.

Then, one cold January morning, everything changed. I was working in recruitment at the time, conducting virtual interviews for a fresh round of hires. My first call of the day was with a young graduate.

As the call began, I couldn't help but notice the loud hum of a fan in the background. It was so distracting that I finally asked, "Why do you have that fan on so loud? It's January, I'm freezing, and you're bundled up in what looks like five layers of clothing."

The young man hesitated for a moment, then replied softly, "Sir, my father owns a small electronics shop, and this laptop is very old. He found it in scrap, repaired it, and gave it to me. If I move away from the fan, the laptop might overheat and shut off during the interview."

I paused. His voice carried no shame, only quiet dignity. There was something about the way he spoke that made me lean in. As we continued the interview, I was struck by his brilliance. Despite the odds, he had earned scholarships, won accolades, and demonstrated an extraordinary depth of knowledge.

Toward the end of the call, curiosity got the better of me. I asked, "Why did you choose to study engineering?"

He paused, and then, with calm determination, he said, "My father is a genius when it comes to electronics, but because he doesn't have a degree, people don't respect his knowledge. My purpose is to earn a degree, not because I believe in its value, but to prove that a degree is just a piece of paper. I want to create something that makes life easier for people like my father, talented and self-taught individuals who aren't recognized because they lack formal education. Money isn't my intent. My intent is to prove that talent deserves respect, regardless of credentials."

His words hit me like a thunderclap. Here was someone whose entire life was guided by intent and purpose. He had clarity. He had direction. Meanwhile, I had spent years drifting, making decisions out of convenience, and letting the tides of circumstance carry me wherever they pleased.

That conversation didn't just linger, it consumed me. For days, I replayed his words in my mind, questioning everything about my own life. What was I doing? Why was I doing it? What impact was I making? I had been running on autopilot for so long, I didn't even know what it felt like to steer.

For the first time, I saw the truth: living without purpose is a kind of quiet self-betrayal. The heaviness I had been feeling wasn't about my job or my degree, it was about the absence of intent. I wasn't building anything. I wasn't contributing to anything. I was simply existing.

That realization lit a fire in me. I began devouring books on psychology, fulfilment, and human behavior. I watched interviews with thought leaders, explored frameworks for finding purpose, and reflected deeply on what truly mattered to me. Slowly, piece by piece, I began to understand.

My purpose wasn't about pay checks, promotions, or prestige. It was about helping others find their own intent and align their lives with their values.

Over the years, I've mentored thousands of people, students, professionals, entrepreneurs, and founders. I've helped them move from confusion to clarity, from drifting to living with purpose. Along the way, I developed strategies and frameworks to transform work from a source of stress into a source of meaning.

This book is my way of sharing those lessons. It's a guide for anyone who feels stuck, lost, or unfulfilled in their work. It's a roadmap to building a career or business where pay checks are just a byproduct of purpose-driven intent.

Because at the end of the day, life is too short to chase "empty pay checks."

Why I Wrote This Book

When I look back at the choices, I made early in my career, one truth stands out, most of those decisions lacked "intent" or "purpose." I followed paths that seemed logical, safe, or socially acceptable, without asking the most important questions: *Why am I doing this? What do I truly care about? What impact do I want to make?*

The years I spent drifting, taught me one crucial lesson. Without purpose, even the most seemingly successful careers can feel hollow. I didn't write this book to tell you what career to choose or how to follow trends. I wrote this book because I know how it feels to wake up each morning with a weight on your chest, knowing you're spending your days working for something that doesn't resonate with you.

This book is the guide I wish I had during those years of confusion, frustration, and self-doubt. It's about helping you discover your "why," align your work with your values, and build a life where fulfilment and intent take centre stage.

The Hidden Costs of Chasing Success Without Purpose

In a world that glorifies hustle and celebrates titles, it's easy to lose sight of what really matters. We're told that success is defined by pay checks, promotions, and prestige. But what we aren't told are the hidden costs of chasing success without purpose:

- **Emotional Burnout**: When your work isn't aligned with your values, every task feels heavier, every challenge feels insurmountable, and even your accomplishments feel empty.

- **Lost Time**: Years can slip by while you're climbing a ladder that's leaning against the wrong wall. By the time you realize it, you might wonder how much time you've wasted chasing someone else's version of success.

- **Eroded Confidence:** Without purpose to anchor you, setbacks feel like failures, and achievements often feel undeserved. The longer you go without direction, the harder it becomes to trust your own choices.

These costs don't just impact your career, they seep into every part of your life, affecting your relationships, your health, and your sense of self-worth.

But it doesn't have to be this way. Work can be more than a paycheck, more than a title, more than a means to an end. Work can be a source of meaning, a platform for impact, and a reflection of who you are and what you stand for.

How This Book Will Guide You Toward Meaningful Work

This book is not a "how-to guide" for chasing trends or maximizing productivity. It's not about working harder or longer or faster. Instead, this book will challenge you to step back, reflect, and redefine success on your own terms.

Inside, you'll find:

- **Clarity:** Tools and exercises to help you identify your values, understand your strengths, and uncover your "why."

- **Strategies:** Frameworks to align your work with your purpose and make intentional decisions about your career or business.

- **Perspective:** Insights into why traditional career advice often falls short and how to navigate work with a deeper sense of intent.

This book isn't about perfection or quick fixes. It's about creating a foundation for work that feels meaningful, impactful, and aligned with who you are. Whether you're a student figuring out your next step, a professional feeling stuck in a job that doesn't resonate, or an entrepreneur searching for deeper fulfilment, this book will guide you toward work that matters.

Because at the end of the day, life is too short to chase "empty pay checks."

Contents

Part 1: The Problem with Work Today 1
    Chapter 1: The Purpose Deficit 6
    Chapter 2: The Science of Purpose 13
    Chapter 3: Escaping the Career Myths 17

Part 2: Discovering Your Purpose 22
    Chapter 4: Mapping Your Mind for Purpose 25
    Chapter 5: Finding Your Why 33
    Chapter 6: The Zone of Genius 38

Part 3: The Path to Purposeful Work 46
    Chapter 7: Setting Intentional Goals 48
    Chapter 8: Purposeful Transitions 56
    Chapter 9: Building Meaning into Your Work Today 66

Part 4: The Toolkit for Intentionality 73
    Chapter 10: The Power of Reflection 76
    Chapter 11: Designing Your Purpose Ecosystem 85
    Chapter 12: Overcoming Resistance 92

Part 5: Managing Challenges on
the Path to Purpose 99
    Chapter 13: Beyond the Breaking Point: How Work
    Challenges Shape Purpose and Performance 102

Chapter 14: Breaking Through Barriers: A Step-by-Step Guide
to Managing Purposeful Challenges 114

Part 6: Lifelong Purpose Evolution 134

Chapter 18: Reimagining Purpose at Midlife 137

Chapter 19: The Spiritual Journey to Purpose 150

Chapter 20: Transcending Materialism 166

Chapter 21: Redefining Work and Success 172

Moving Beyond the Paycheck and Building
Your Purpose Legacy 178

Bonus Resources: Tools to Build Your Purpose Ecosystem . 192

Final Thoughts 202

About the Author 203

Book Summary 205

Part 1

The Problem with Work Today

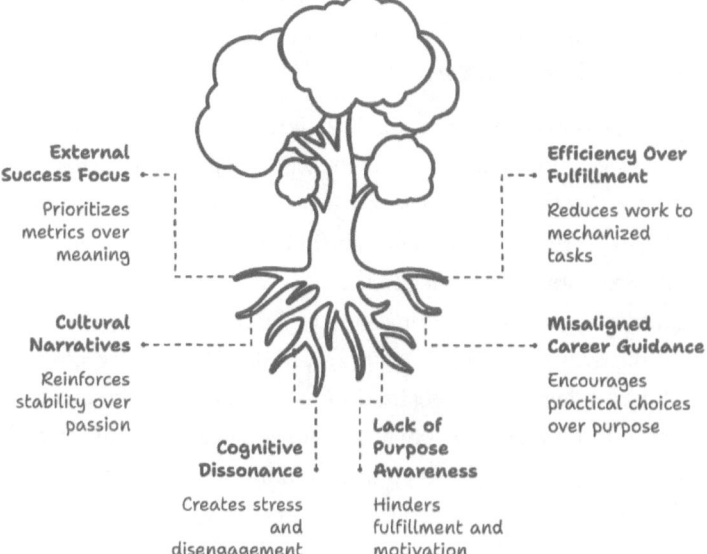

Purpose Deficit in Modern Work

External Success Focus
Prioritizes metrics over meaning

Cultural Narratives
Reinforces stability over passion

Cognitive Dissonance
Creates stress and disengagement

Lack of Purpose Awareness
Hinders fulfillment and motivation

Efficiency Over Fulfillment
Reduces work to mechanized tasks

Misaligned Career Guidance
Encourages practical choices over purpose

The world of work is in a quiet crisis. Beneath the hustle and ambition lies a pervasive sense of dissatisfaction, a gnawing feeling that something isn't quite right. Many careers, despite being successful on the surface, feel unfulfilling. Even as people climb higher on the corporate ladder, achieve professional accolades, or secure financial stability, a deeper question lingers: *Why does this still feel empty?*

The answer lies in a fundamental disconnect between what we do and why we do it. The modern workplace often prioritizes efficiency, output, and external metrics of success, factors that, while important, rarely satisfy our deeper need for purpose. The result is a workforce filled with individuals who are highly capable but emotionally disengaged, doing work that pays the bills but doesn't fill the soul.

The roots of this crisis run deep. Historical and cultural forces have shaped how we think about work, embedding myths and expectations that no longer serve us. The industrial revolution turned work into a mechanized, impersonal process, reducing labor to tasks and outputs. In the 20th century, corporate culture built on this foundation, creating systems that prioritized productivity over people. And now, in the 21st century, the rise of technology and globalization has brought unprecedented opportunities but also new pressures, constant connectivity, blurred boundaries between work and life, and a relentless push for more.

The result is what some have called the "Purpose Deficit," a widespread lack of alignment between people's work and their deeper values and aspirations. This deficit manifests in subtle but powerful ways: a sense of detachment, a loss of enthusiasm, and a creeping dread that makes Monday mornings feel like an insurmountable hurdle. The Purpose Deficit isn't just a personal problem; it's a systemic issue that affects organizations, communities, and economies. Disengaged workers are less innovative, less productive, and more likely to burn out, costing billions in lost potential every year.

But the Purpose Deficit is not inevitable. It's the product of outdated ideas about work, ideas that can and must be challenged. To understand the problem with work today, we need to explore the societal forces that shape our career choices, the psychological costs of misaligned work, and the myths that keep people trapped in unfulfilling roles.

Why Work Feels Unfulfilling

At its core, the dissatisfaction many people feel with their careers comes from a lack of alignment. Purposeful work is work that connects what you do with what you care about. It's work that reflects your values, uses your strengths, and contributes to something meaningful. But the structures and systems of modern work often make this kind of alignment difficult.

One reason is the focus on external markers of success. From an early age, we're taught that work is about achieving certain milestones: earning a degree, landing a prestigious job, climbing the corporate ladder. These markers are tangible and measurable, but they rarely reflect the full spectrum of what makes work meaningful. As a result, many people find themselves pursuing goals that look good on paper but feel hollow in practice.

Another reason is the way work has been structured to prioritize efficiency over fulfillment. In many organizations, tasks are broken down into repetitive, mechanized processes designed to maximize output. This approach might work well for manufacturing, but it's ill-suited for the complexities of human motivation. People thrive when they feel connected to their work, when they see how their efforts contribute to something bigger. Without that connection, even the most competent employees can feel disengaged.

The Societal Pressures That Shape Work

Cultural narratives play a significant role in perpetuating the Purpose Deficit. These narratives tell us that work should be hard, that stability is more important than fulfillment, and that success is measured by wealth or status. They discourage exploration and experimentation, pushing people toward predictable paths that feel safe but uninspired.

Parents, teachers, and peers often reinforce these narratives, not out of malice but out of concern. They encourage young people to pursue "practical" careers, to choose stability over passion, and to prioritize financial security. While these priorities are understandable, they often leave little room for purpose. The result is a generation of workers who feel stuck in careers that don't reflect who they are or what they want.

The Psychological Costs of Misaligned Work

The Purpose Deficit isn't just a philosophical issue; it's a psychological one. Misaligned work creates what psychologists call cognitive dissonance, the mental discomfort that arises when your actions don't match your values. This dissonance can lead to stress, anxiety, and a sense of emptiness that's hard to shake. Over time, it can erode motivation, engagement, and even physical health.

Research shows that people who feel a strong sense of purpose are not only more satisfied with their work but also more resilient in the face of challenges. They're less likely to experience burnout, more likely to perform at a high level, and more likely to stay engaged over the long term. Purpose isn't just a nice-to-have; it's a key driver of well-being and success.

The Way Forward

Understanding the problem with work today is the first step toward addressing it. The Purpose Deficit is not inevitable, it's the product of systems and narratives that can be changed. By challenging outdated ideas about success, prioritizing alignment over output, and creating environments that support purposeful work, we can build careers that feel fulfilling, not just functional.

In the chapters ahead, we'll explore how to uncover your unique purpose, navigate the myths that keep people trapped in unfulfilling roles, and create a path to work that aligns with your values and aspirations. Because the problem with work today isn't just that it's broken, it's that it can be so much more.

Chapter 1

The Purpose Deficit

When Andrew Carnegie sold his steel empire in 1901, he became one of the wealthiest men in history. On the surface, his life seemed like the epitome of success, a man who had built an industrial empire from scratch, climbing to the pinnacle of wealth and power. But beneath the glittering achievements lay a profound realization: his success had not brought him fulfillment. Carnegie, who had spent decades pursuing wealth, famously declared, "The man who dies rich dies disgraced." It was a stark acknowledgment that purpose, not profit, was the true measure of a life well lived. His story is a vivid reminder that external rewards, no matter how grand, often fail to fill the internal void left by a lack of alignment between what we do and why we do it.

This void, the Purpose Deficit, isn't exclusive to the wealthy and powerful. It's an experience that touches millions of people in countless industries, professions, and walks of life. It's what happens when work becomes an obligation rather than a source of meaning. It's the quiet dissatisfaction that creeps in when we realize that the ladder we've been climbing might be leaning against the wrong wall. The Purpose Deficit isn't just about feeling unmotivated or disengaged; it's about the fundamental disconnect between external achievements and internal fulfillment.

To understand why the Purpose Deficit is so pervasive, we have to look beyond individual experiences and explore the psychological and systemic forces shaping how we approach work and success. Psychologists often describe purpose as the alignment of values, actions, and impact. When these three elements come together, work feels meaningful and rewarding. But when they are out of sync, when our actions don't reflect our values or when our work doesn't create the impact, we care about, the result is a profound sense of disconnection. This is where the Purpose Deficit begins.

A key factor in the Purpose Deficit is the cultural narrative around success. From a young age, we are taught to focus on external markers of achievement, grades, accolades, job titles, and salaries. These metrics are easy to measure, easy to compare, and easy to chase, which makes them alluring. But they are often detached from the deeper question of why we do what we do? Carnegie's story is an extreme example of this. By all conventional measures, he was wildly successful, but it wasn't until he turned his attention to philanthropy that he felt a sense of purpose. His life reveals a simple but profound truth: external success without internal alignment is a hollow victory.

The Purpose Deficit is not just a personal struggle; it's also deeply rooted in systemic forces. Consider the concept of deficit thinking, a mindset that attributes failure or shortcomings to personal inadequacies rather than systemic issues. In many professional settings, individuals are constantly told to focus on their weaknesses, to "fix" what's wrong with them, rather than recognizing and building on their strengths. This narrative, whether intentional or not, reinforces a sense of inadequacy. It shifts attention away from the structural factors that contribute to dissatisfaction, such as unrealistic expectations, toxic work cultures, or societal pressures, and places the burden squarely on the individual. Over time, this can erode confidence and make purpose feel elusive, even unattainable.

Another lens through which to view the Purpose Deficit is existential psychology, which frames the search for meaning as a fundamental aspect of human existence. Existential thinkers argue that purpose isn't something we find passively, it's something we actively create. This perspective introduces two daunting but empowering realities: freedom and responsibility. Freedom means rejecting the scripts handed to us by society, family, or employers and defining success on our own terms. Responsibility means taking ownership of that definition and the choices that flow from it. Both are difficult. It's far easier to follow a well-trodden path, even if it leads to dissatisfaction, than to face the uncertainty of forging your own.

This dynamic plays out in countless workplaces every day. Employees take on roles that look good on paper, driven by promises of stability, status, or financial security. At first, the external rewards provide a sense of validation. A promotion, a raise, a corner office, all of these can feel like proof that we're on the right track. But over time, the excitement fades, leaving behind a lingering question: Is this it? The phenomenon of hedonic adaptation explains why this happens. External rewards provide a temporary boost in happiness, but their effects wear off quickly, leaving us craving the next big achievement. Without a deeper sense of purpose to anchor us, we end up stuck on a treadmill, running faster but going nowhere.

The human psyche is not wired to thrive on external rewards alone. Research shows that people are most engaged and fulfilled when their work aligns with their intrinsic motivations, curiosity, growth, contribution. Viktor Frankl, a Holocaust survivor and psychiatrist, captured this idea powerfully in his book *Man's*

Search for Meaning. Frankl observed that even in the most harrowing circumstances, individuals who found meaning in their suffering were able to endure and even thrive. His insights remind us that purpose is not a luxury; it's a necessity. It's what sustains us in the face of challenges and gives our efforts a sense of direction and significance.

The Purpose Deficit often masquerades as practicality. It tells us to prioritize what's safe, predictable, or expected. It whispers that purpose is a nice-to-have, not a must-have. But history and psychology tell a different story. Purpose is not an indulgence; it's the foundation of meaningful work and a fulfilling life. Without it, even the most impressive achievements feel hollow. With it, even the most challenging endeavours become worthwhile.

The cost of the Purpose Deficit isn't always immediate or obvious. It's not like a broken leg that forces you to stop and acknowledge the pain. It's more like a slow, creeping fatigue that you get used to over time, convincing yourself it's just part of life. You keep going, after all, everyone else seems to be doing the same, until one day you wake up and realize you've been running on empty for years.

This subtle erosion often begins with disconnection. You might start to feel emotionally detached from your work, going through the motions without really engaging. Tasks that once seemed exciting now feel like chores. Even the wins, the moments that are supposed to feel like milestones, your promotion, your performance bonus, your name on the team leader board, start to ring hollow. And then there's the dread. It creeps in on Sunday evenings, lingers through your commute, and sits heavily on your chest every Monday morning.

But here's the twist: even in the midst of all this, you might convince yourself that you're fine. The Purpose Deficit has a way of disguising itself as practicality. "I'm just paying my dues," you tell yourself. "This is what being responsible looks like." These justifications are comforting in the short term, but over time, they can become barriers to change. They keep you tethered to work that doesn't fulfill you, feeding the very cycle of disconnection you're trying to escape.

The psychological impact of this disconnection goes deeper than just dissatisfaction. Psychologists call it cognitive dissonance, the mental discomfort that arises when your actions are out of sync with your values. For example, if you value creativity but spend your days stuck in a rigid, process-driven role, or if you care deeply about social impact but work for an organization whose priorities are purely profit-driven, that misalignment creates tension. It's like living in a house where the foundation is slightly off-kilter. At first, it's barely noticeable. But over time, the cracks begin to show.

Cognitive dissonance doesn't just affect your mind; it seeps into your body as well. Studies have shown that chronic misalignment between values and actions can lead to increased stress, burnout, and even physical health problems. The body keeps score, as they say. And while stress is often framed as a necessary byproduct of ambition, the kind of stress that comes from the Purpose Deficit isn't productive, it's corrosive.

Consider the example of John Stuart Mill, the 19th-century philosopher and economist. Mill was a prodigy, educated rigorously by his father and hailed as one of the brightest minds of his time. By the age of 20, he was already a leading figure in intellectual circles. But despite his remarkable achievements, Mill fell into a deep depression. His life, which seemed so successful on the surface, felt empty. "I seemed to have nothing left to live for," he later wrote. It wasn't until he shifted his focus from abstract intellectual pursuits to issues of social reform, work that aligned with his values, that Mill began to feel a renewed sense of purpose.

Mill's story illustrates a fundamental truth about purpose: it's not optional. It's not a luxury to pursue when everything else is in order. It's a cornerstone of mental and emotional well-being. Without it, even the brightest achievements can feel meaningless.

Another facet of the Purpose Deficit is its impact on identity. In many ways, our work shapes how we see ourselves. It gives us a sense of place in the world, a way to answer the question, "What do you do?" But when the work we do doesn't align with who we are, that question can feel like a trap. You might feel like an imposter, going through the motions of a role that doesn't reflect your true self. Or you might feel fragmented, as though there's a gap between the version of you that shows up at work and the version of you that exists in your mind.

This fragmentation can be particularly challenging in a culture that equates busyness with worth. We've been conditioned to believe that being productive, efficient, and constantly occupied is a badge of honor. But what happens when all that busyness starts to feel like motion without meaning? What happens when you realize you've been working hard, but not working toward anything that really matters to you? These moments of reckoning can be unsettling, but they're also essential. They're the cracks that let the light in.

Recognizing the Purpose Deficit isn't about self-blame. It's not about beating yourself up for the choices you've made or the paths you've taken. It's about understanding the systemic, cultural, and psychological forces that shape our approach to work, and then deciding how to move forward. Purpose isn't something you find by accident. It's something you cultivate through intention, reflection, and the willingness to make changes when things aren't working.

It requires us to confront the uncomfortable truths about our choices, our motivations, and the narratives we've internalized. But it's also an opportunity, a chance to realign our actions with our values, to redefine success on our own terms, and to create a career and life that resonate deeply with who we are. Purpose isn't something we stumble upon; it's something we build, piece by piece, through the decisions we make every day.

In the next section, we'll begin to explore how to identify the signs of the Purpose Deficit in your own life and take the first steps toward realignment. It's not an easy process, but it's one worth undertaking. Because at the end of the day, life isn't about ticking boxes or meeting quotas. It's about finding work that resonates with your values, your aspirations, and your sense of self.

Chapter 2

The Science of Purpose

The concept of purpose has been central to human thought for millennia, evolving through philosophy, psychology, and science. It has shaped how we understand fulfillment, happiness, and the meaning of life. While modern conversations about purpose often focus on career alignment or personal fulfillment, the roots of this idea run deeper, offering profound insights into what it means to live a meaningful life.

Purpose has always been about alignment, the connection between what you value, what you do, and the impact you aim to make. This connection is not a luxury or an afterthought; it is fundamental to our psychological, emotional, and even biological well-being. Understanding the evolution of purpose, from ancient philosophies to contemporary science, reveals its timeless importance and practical relevance in our lives today.

The ancient Greeks were among the first to formalize the concept of purpose. Aristotle introduced *eudaimonia*, often translated as "flourishing" or "the good life." For Aristotle, purpose was not about fleeting happiness or external rewards but about fulfilling one's potential through virtuous living and rational action. He believed that true purpose arose from aligning one's actions with one's character, striving toward excellence in both thought and behavior. Aristotle's vision of purpose emphasized that meaning comes from the choices we make and the values we embody.

Stoic philosophers like Epictetus and Seneca expanded on this idea, focusing on resilience and self-discipline as pathways to purpose. For the Stoics, purpose wasn't dependent on external circumstances, which were often beyond one's control. Instead, it was rooted in how one chose to respond to life's challenges. They believed that by living in harmony with nature and reason, individuals could find meaning even in adversity. Their insights remind us that purpose isn't always tied to grand achievements, it can be found in the quiet strength of persevering through difficulty and staying true to one's principles.

In modern times, the exploration of purpose moved from philosophical thought to scientific inquiry, offering new dimensions to our understanding of this deeply human pursuit. Viktor Frankl, a Holocaust survivor and psychiatrist, profoundly shaped modern discussions of purpose with his concept of logotherapy. Frankl observed that the search for meaning was the primary driver of human behavior. Even in the unimaginable suffering of a concentration camp, he found that those who could identify a purpose, a reason to endure, were more resilient. His famous insight, "Those who have a 'why' to live can bear almost any 'how,'" highlights the transformative power of purpose in navigating life's most challenging moments.

Purpose also gained empirical grounding through psychological research. Edward Deci and Richard Ryan's Self-Determination Theory (SDT) identified autonomy, competence, and relatedness as fundamental psychological needs that drive intrinsic motivation. When these needs are met, individuals are more likely to experience a sense of purpose. Purposeful work often aligns with these needs, offering freedom to make meaningful choices, opportunities to excel, and connections that foster a sense of belonging. This explains why purpose feels energizing, it satisfies the very core of what makes us human.

The impact of purpose extends beyond motivation and fulfillment, it reaches into our biology. Neuroscience has revealed that engaging in purposeful activities activates the brain's reward system, releasing dopamine and enhancing focus, resilience, and satisfaction. This biological response explains why work that aligns with our values feels invigorating, while purposeless tasks drain us. Over time, the absence of purpose triggers stress responses, leading to burnout, a state not just of exhaustion but of existential disconnection. Purpose, in this sense, is not optional; it is essential for sustaining energy and well-being.

Recent research takes this understanding further, showing how purpose arises from the interplay of biological, psychological, and social factors. This biopsychosocial perspective highlights that purpose is both deeply personal and profoundly influenced by our environment. It is shaped by our individual values and aspirations, but also by the stories we inherit, the communities we engage with, and the opportunities we encounter. Purpose, then, is not static, it is dynamic, evolving with our experiences and circumstances.

Purpose is also gaining recognition in organizational contexts, where its collective dimension comes into play. Companies that align their missions with broader societal values often report greater employee engagement, loyalty, and long-term success. This mirrors what individuals experience on a smaller scale: when personal values resonate with larger goals, the result is a sense of alignment that fuels both fulfillment and productivity. Purpose, whether individual or collective, creates a positive feedback loop, each success reinforces the motivation to continue pursuing meaningful work.

But purpose is not just about grand ideas or large-scale change. It is about the small, deliberate actions that bring our lives closer to alignment. Purpose is not something you find; it is something you create, through reflection, experimentation, and persistence. It is less about discovering a singular "why" and more about continually asking, *what matters to me now? How can I act on it?* The pursuit of purpose is not a destination, it is a lifelong practice.

The science of purpose reminds us that meaning is not handed to us. It is built through the choices we make and the lives we lead. Purpose does not require extraordinary circumstances or talents, it requires clarity, intention, and a willingness to act. As we move forward, we will examine the myths that keep people from pursuing purposeful work and the tools we can use to break free from them. Because understanding the science of purpose is only the beginning, the real transformation comes when we use this understanding to shape lives and careers that truly resonate.

Chapter 3

Escaping the Career Myths

The myths surrounding careers often feel as immovable as mountains, handed down through generations, reinforced by societal expectations, and embedded in the cultural fabric of success. They tell us that careers should follow predictable paths, that passion will magically guide us, that stability is the ultimate goal, and that external markers like titles and paychecks define our worth. But these myths, comforting as they may seem, often trap us in cycles of dissatisfaction, misalignment, and regret. Escaping them is not just about rejecting these narratives; it's about actively constructing new ones that align with purpose, growth, and fulfillment.

Breaking free from career myths requires more than just recognition of their existence. It involves understanding the deeper forces that shape career decisions and applying strategies rooted in evidence-based theories to align work with your evolving self-concept, values, and aspirations.

Donald Super's Developmental Self-Concept Theory offers a foundational perspective on why careers feel dynamic and personal. Super argued that career development is a lifelong process, shaped by an evolving sense of self. According to this theory, people move through distinct stages in their careers: growth, exploration, establishment, maintenance, and decline. Each stage reflects changes in self-concept, interests, and values. For example, in the growth phase, you might follow societal expectations to establish your career, but in later stages, you might prioritize roles that align with deeper personal fulfillment. This perspective allows for fluidity, showing that it's not only okay but essential to reassess and realign as you mature. Recognizing your career as a reflection of your evolving self can help you reject rigid myths and embrace purposeful transitions.

Building on Super's work, Mark Savickas' Career Construction Theory emphasizes the narratives we tell about our work. According to this theory, careers are not static, they are stories we actively construct. This means that the way you frame your experiences, challenges, and aspirations shapes how you perceive your career path. For example, instead of seeing a career pivot as a failure to stay on a linear path, you might reframe it as an exploration of your values and an opportunity to discover meaningful work. By actively rewriting your career story, you can escape myths that bind you to outdated expectations and craft a narrative that aligns with your purpose.

Albert Bandura's Social Cognitive Career Theory provides a practical framework for overcoming the limiting beliefs that career myths instill. Central to this theory is the concept of self-efficacy, the belief in your ability to succeed in specific tasks or roles. Many myths, like the fear of instability or the idea that success only comes from traditional paths, erode self-efficacy, making it harder to pursue purpose-driven careers. Bandura's theory emphasizes the importance of positive reinforcement, mentorship, and learning experiences in building self-efficacy. For example, seeking mentorship can provide not only guidance but also validation that your aspirations are achievable. By cultivating confidence in your abilities, you're more likely to break free from myths and pursue work that reflects your values.

John Krumboltz's Social Learning Theory shifts the focus from fixed traits to lifelong adaptability. According to this theory, career decisions are shaped by the experiences you encounter, not predetermined by personality or early choices. This perspective encourages exploration, experimentation, and openness to change. Instead of feeling constrained by past decisions or societal expectations, Krumboltz's approach reminds us that purpose evolves as we grow. For example, if you once pursued a career for its stability but now feel unfulfilled, this theory supports the idea that your interests and skills can change, and that's not a failure but an opportunity.

An emerging framework, Purpose-Centered Career Development, integrates these insights into a cohesive approach focused on identifying and leveraging personal strengths and values. This model emphasizes that purpose isn't something you find; it's something you create by aligning your work with what gives you meaning. By identifying what energizes and fulfills you, this framework guides you toward careers that resonate deeply with your sense of purpose.

To put these theories into practice, consider strategies that help dismantle career myths and create pathways to more meaningful work:

1. **Self-Reflection:** Regular self-reflection is essential. Ask yourself: *What do I value most? What impact do I want to have? What brings me energy and fulfillment?* Understanding your values, strengths, and interests provides a foundation for aligning your work with your purpose.

2. **Explore Diverse Opportunities:** Myths often confine us to narrow definitions of success, but purpose thrives in exploration. Allow yourself to try different roles,

industries, or projects. Experimentation is not a lack of direction, it's a deliberate way to uncover what resonates with you.

3. **Seek Mentorship:** Mentors offer more than guidance; they provide perspective. Finding someone who has navigated unconventional paths or pursued purpose-driven work can challenge myths and expand your sense of what's possible.

4. **Reframe Your Narrative:** Using the principles of Career Construction Theory, rewrite your career story. Instead of seeing setbacks or pivots as failures, frame them as steps in your journey toward alignment and growth. Your narrative is yours to shape, make it one that inspires and empowers you.

5. **Embrace Lifelong Learning:** Skills and interests evolve, and careers should too. Committing to continuous learning, whether through formal education, new experiences, or self-directed exploration, keeps you adaptable and open to new opportunities that align with your purpose.

Breaking free from career myths requires a willingness to question deeply held beliefs and take action toward building a life that feels authentic. It means rejecting the idea that there's only one right path and embracing the idea that careers, like people, are dynamic and ever-changing. By applying these strategies and drawing from the theories of career development, you can begin to dismantle the myths that hold you back and build a career rooted in purpose.

This journey isn't about arriving at a single, perfect destination. It's about cultivating alignment between who you are, what you value, and the work you do. Purpose isn't static; it's a relationship between you and your evolving aspirations. In the next chapter, we'll delve into practical frameworks for uncovering your unique purpose and mapping the path toward work that truly resonates.

Part 2

Discovering Your Purpose

Unveiling the Path to Purpose

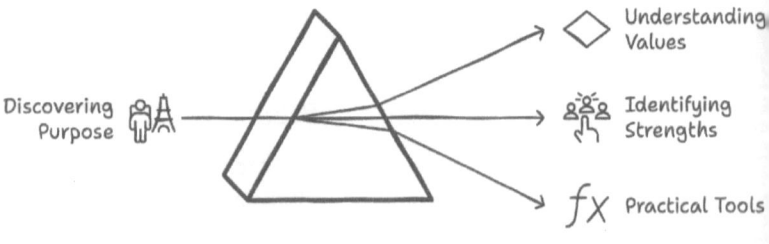

Purpose is not a luxury; it is a necessity. It is the quiet force that gives our actions meaning, the compass that directs us when external markers of success fall short. Yet, for many, the path to discovering purpose feels elusive, obscured by societal expectations, personal doubts, and the noise of a world that prioritizes productivity over meaning.

This section is about cutting through that noise. It's about shifting the focus inward, examining who you are at your core, and uncovering what drives you. Purpose isn't something you stumble upon, it's something you actively cultivate. It grows from self-awareness, curiosity, and a willingness to challenge the stories you've been told about work and success.

The process of discovering your purpose begins with understanding your values. Values are the foundation of purpose, the principles that guide your decisions and shape your priorities. When your work aligns with your values, it feels energizing and meaningful. When it doesn't, even the most lucrative or prestigious careers can feel empty.

But values alone are not enough. Discovering purpose also requires understanding your strengths, the skills, talents, and passions that make you unique. It's about identifying the activities that make you lose track of time, the problems you enjoy solving, and the contributions that bring you a sense of pride. Purpose often lies at the intersection of values and strengths, where what you care about meets what you're good at.

This section will guide you through practical tools and frameworks for uncovering your purpose. You'll learn how to map your mind, explore your "why," and step into your Zone of Genius, the space where your talents and passions converge to create work that feels not just productive, but deeply fulfilling. We'll also address the fears and doubts that arise during this process, providing strategies to overcome resistance and take meaningful action.

Discovering your purpose is not about perfection or certainty. It's about progress. It's about taking small, intentional steps toward alignment, allowing your purpose to evolve as you grow. Whether you're at the start of your career, considering a major pivot, or simply looking to deepen the meaning in your work, this section will help you lay the groundwork for a life and career built on purpose.

Chapter 4

Mapping Your Mind for Purpose

Mapping your mind for purpose is not a vague exercise in self-reflection; it's a deliberate, structured process that requires digging deep into your values, strengths, motivations, and the stories you tell yourself about work and success. It's about creating a mental blueprint that aligns who you are with what you do and identifying the gaps that leave you feeling unfulfilled. This chapter provides a step-by-step framework to uncover the drivers of meaningful work and create a foundation for purpose-driven decision-making.

At the heart of this process is the understanding that purpose is deeply personal. It is not dictated by societal norms, family expectations, or corporate milestones. Purpose is rooted in the alignment between your internal drivers, what you value and what energizes you, and your external actions. To map your mind for purpose, you must first clear away the clutter of inherited beliefs and career myths that distort your view of what success should look like.

The starting point is **self-concept**, a key idea from Donald Super's Developmental Self-Concept Theory. Super argued that your career is not a static choice but a dynamic journey shaped by how you see yourself. Mapping your mind for purpose requires revisiting this self-concept regularly. Begin by asking: *How do I define myself today? What roles, professional or personal, feel most authentic to me? What parts of my identity are being* *underutilized or ignored in my current work?* This exercise reveals the disconnects that may be holding you back from work that resonates with your evolving self.

Next, explore your **values**, which act as the compass guiding your decisions. Values are non-negotiable principles that determine what matters most to you, whether it's creativity, autonomy, impact, or security. Start by listing what you believe to be your core values, then rank them in order of importance. Now, assess how your current work aligns with these values. For example, if you value creativity but work in a role that prioritizes rigid processes, the misalignment will feel draining over time. Conversely, if your work allows you to express your top values consistently, you're more likely to feel energized and fulfilled.

Building on this foundation, turn your attention to **strengths**. Strengths are not just the skills you're good at but the ones that give you energy when you use them. They often overlap with what psychologists call *signature strengths*, the abilities that feel most natural to you and that others recognize as your unique contributions. To identify these, think about the tasks or projects where time seems to disappear, those moments of "flow" when you're fully engaged. Ask yourself: *What do I excel at that also excites me? What feedback do I consistently receive from others about my contributions?* Mapping your strengths is crucial because purpose lies at the intersection of what you value and what you're skilled at.

Now, dig into your **motivations**. Unlike values, which are enduring principles, motivations are dynamic, they change based on context, experience, and aspirations. Use tools like journaling or mind mapping to reflect on what drives you today. Consider these questions: *What motivates me to get out of bed in the morning? Is it the impact I'm making, the relationships I'm building, or the skills*

I'm developing? What feels missing in my current work? By identifying your motivations, you can pinpoint the gaps that leave you feeling unfulfilled and begin to address them.

An often-overlooked but critical part of mapping your mind is examining the **stories you tell yourself** about work and success. This idea, central to Mark Savickas' Career Construction Theory, suggests that your career narrative shapes your decisions and perceptions. For example, if you view a past career pivot as a failure, you might hesitate to take risks or explore new paths. But if you reframe that pivot as a bold step toward alignment, it becomes a source of strength and clarity. Reflect on the stories you've internalized about your career and ask: *Are they serving me, or are they limiting me? How can I rewrite these stories to better reflect my values and aspirations?*

Finally, mapping your mind for purpose requires an **iterative approach**. Purpose is not a fixed destination but an evolving process. This aligns with John Krumboltz's Social Learning Theory, which emphasizes adaptability and learning from experience. To put this into practice, experiment with small changes that align your work with your values and strengths. For instance, if you value connection but work in a solitary role, seek opportunities to collaborate with colleagues or build relationships within your industry. Treat these experiments as low-risk opportunities to test what feels right, adjusting your approach as you learn more about yourself.

Here's how to tie it all together into an actionable framework for mapping your mind:

1. Define Your Self-Concept

Your self-concept is the foundation of your purpose map. It's how you see yourself, both professionally and personally, and how you envision your future self. To define your self-concept:

- **Reflect deeply:** Begin by writing a description of who you are today. Be honest and specific. For example, "I'm a detail-oriented problem solver who thrives in structured environments but feels creatively stifled in my current role."

- **Visualize your future self:** Write down how you want to evolve. Consider the qualities, roles, and contributions you aspire to embody. For instance, "I want to be a leader who uses creativity and strategy to build innovative teams."

- **Identify gaps:** Compare your current self-concept to your future vision. Where are the disconnects? What qualities, skills, or opportunities do you need to cultivate to bridge those gaps?

This exercise helps you clarify your identity and the direction you want to grow. It also provides a reference point for evaluating whether your current path aligns with your aspirations.

2. Clarify Your Values

Values are your guiding principles, the non-negotiables that define what matters most to you. To clarify your values:

- **Create a values inventory:** Write down as many values as you can think of, examples include creativity, autonomy, collaboration, impact, and security.

- **Prioritize them:** Narrow your list to your top five values and rank them by importance. For example, you might rank autonomy as your top value, followed by creativity, collaboration, impact, and growth.

- **Compare your values to your current work:** Reflect on whether your current role honors your values. For example, if autonomy is your highest priority but your work involves constant micromanagement, that misalignment is a red flag.

Understanding your values allows you to make decisions that align with your deepest priorities. It also helps you identify areas of misalignment, guiding you toward changes that feel meaningful and authentic.

3. Identify Your Strengths

Your strengths are not just skills; they're the tasks and activities that make you feel energized and confident. To identify your strengths:

- **Reflect on your "flow" moments:** Think of times when you were so absorbed in a task that you lost track of time. What were you doing? What aspects of that work felt natural and rewarding?

- **Seek external feedback:** Ask trusted colleagues, mentors, or friends to describe what they see as your greatest strengths. Often, others notice abilities we overlook.

- **Validate your strengths through patterns:** Look for recurring themes in your reflections and feedback. For example, if both your reflections and external feedback highlight your ability to simplify complex ideas, that's a signature strength.

Strengths are key to purpose because they point to the kinds of work you're not only good at but also enjoy. Aligning your work with your strengths creates a sense of fulfillment and flow.

4. Assess Your Motivations

Motivations are the drivers behind your actions. Unlike values, which are more stable, motivations can shift depending on your context and goals. To assess your motivations:

- **Identify what excites you:** Think about the tasks or aspects of your work that you look forward to. What gives you energy and satisfaction?

- **Acknowledge what drains you:** Be honest about the parts of your work that feel like a chore or sap your energy.

- **Look for patterns:** Are you motivated by growth and learning? By making an impact? By recognition or autonomy? Write down your observations.

Understanding your motivations helps you identify the elements of work that keep you engaged and the aspects that need to change. It also clarifies whether your current role aligns with what drives you.

5. Rewrite Your Career Narrative

The stories you tell yourself about your career shape your decisions and perceptions. To rewrite your narrative:

- **Identify limiting beliefs:** Write down the negative or constraining stories you've internalized. For example, "I can't change careers now because I'm too far along in this path."

- **Reframe these beliefs:** Replace limiting narratives with empowering ones. For example, "My previous experiences have given me unique skills that I can bring to a new path."

- **Craft a forward-looking story:** Write a new career narrative that reflects your values, strengths, and aspirations. For example, "I'm someone who values creativity and autonomy, and I'm taking steps to align my career with these priorities."

Rewriting your narrative helps you break free from myths and expectations that no longer serve you. It allows you to see your career as a dynamic journey rather than a rigid path.

6. Experiment and Adapt

Purpose is not discovered all at once, it's built through exploration and iteration. To experiment and adapt:

- **Test small changes:** Introduce purpose-driven shifts in your current role. For example, propose a project that aligns with your strengths or seek mentorship in an area that excites you.

- **Explore new opportunities:** If your current role offers little room for alignment, explore side projects, volunteer work, or courses that let you test new directions.

- **Reflect on outcomes:** After each experiment, ask yourself: *Did this align with my values? Did it energize me? What did I learn about myself?*

Treat these experiments as data points. Each step, whether successful or not, provides valuable insights that refine your purpose map and guide your next move.

Integrating the Framework

To tie these steps together, create a purpose map that visually represents your reflections:

- Write your self-concept, values, strengths, motivations, and narrative on individual sections of the map.

- Draw connections between them. For example, link your top values to strengths you can use to honor those values or your motivations to specific aspects of your self-concept.

- Identify gaps or areas where alignment is missing. These gaps represent opportunities for growth and exploration.

By following these steps, you create a detailed map of your mind that highlights where you are, where you want to go, and how to get there. Purpose doesn't emerge from passivity; it's built through intentional exploration, reflection, and action. As we move into the next chapter, we'll focus on uncovering your "why," the core driver that gives your map direction and makes your purpose unmistakably your own.

Chapter 5

Finding Your Why

Finding your "why" is a journey into the core of your identity, a process of uncovering the fundamental beliefs, motivations, and values that guide your life. It's a question that transcends what you do and how you do it, asking instead why you do it in the first place. This deeper connection between intention and action creates a foundation for fulfillment, resilience, and impact. Historical examples, scientific insights, and real-world frameworks all underscore the transformative power of finding and living your "why."

Simon Sinek's **Golden Circle** framework provides a powerful lens for understanding the role of purpose in our lives. Sinek highlights three layers of action: "what," the external tasks we perform; "how," the methods and values we apply; and "why," the core belief that drives us. For instance, in the mid-20th century, Dr. Martin Luther King Jr.'s "what" was civil rights activism, his "how" was nonviolent resistance, and his "why" was the fundamental belief in the dignity and equality of all people. By articulating and living his "why," Dr. King inspired a movement that transformed societal norms and laws. His "why" wasn't just a rhetorical device; it was the compass that directed every action, even in the face of immense adversity.

But purpose isn't just philosophical, it's deeply biological. The brain's **reward system** plays a critical role in reinforcing purpose-driven behavior. Dopamine, the neurotransmitter associated with motivation and reward, is released when we engage in actions aligned with our values and aspirations. Historical figures often demonstrate this alignment in their achievements. Consider Marie Curie, who pursued groundbreaking research in radioactivity despite immense societal and financial obstacles. Her "why" was a relentless commitment to scientific discovery and its potential to benefit humanity. The dopamine-driven satisfaction she derived from incremental progress likely sustained her through the challenges of her work, including the personal health risks involved.

The **limbic system**, the brain's emotional core, further underscores the power of purpose. Unlike the neocortex, which handles logic and language, the limbic system governs feelings, intuition, and motivation. This explains why articulating your "why" can be challenging, it's rooted in emotional truths that don't always translate easily into words. For instance, Mahatma Gandhi's "why" of nonviolent resistance stemmed from a profound sense of justice and compassion rather than a logical strategy alone. His intuitive grasp of the emotional and moral dimensions of his mission resonated deeply with millions, transcending language, and culture.

Purpose is not only a psychological anchor but also a source of physical resilience. Research consistently shows that individuals with a strong sense of purpose are better equipped to manage stress and adversity. Viktor Frankl, a Holocaust survivor and author of *Man's Search for Meaning*, exemplifies this truth. While enduring unimaginable suffering in concentration camps, Frankl's "why" was to survive and share his insights on the importance of meaning in life. His belief that purpose could sustain life even in the face of profound suffering became not just his survival mechanism but also his life's work. Frankl's resilience highlights the intersection of psychological purpose and physical endurance.

The brain's **seeking system**, identified by neuroscientist Jaak Panksepp, offers another layer of insight. This system motivates exploration and learning, driving us to pursue goals that align with our values. Historical innovators like Thomas Edison exemplify this principle. Edison's "why" was rooted in a belief that invention could improve everyday life. His seeking system drove relentless experimentation, famously involving over a thousand failed attempts to create the electric light bulb. His "why" sustained his curiosity and determination, ensuring that each failure was seen not as a setback but as a step closer to success.

To uncover your "why," begin with reflective exercises. Consider the moments in your life that felt deeply fulfilling or impactful. For example, if you've consistently felt a sense of purpose when mentoring others, this could point to a "why" centered on empowerment and growth. Reflect on the opposite as well, moments of frustration or disengagement often reveal values that were ignored. For instance, if you've felt unfulfilled in roles that lacked autonomy, your "why" may involve independence and creative freedom.

Historical figures provide illuminating examples of this process. Take Florence Nightingale, whose "why" was to improve healthcare systems and patient outcomes. Her early dissatisfaction with the societal expectations placed on women in her era pushed her to seek a deeper purpose. When she found it in nursing, her "why" became the foundation for her revolutionary contributions to modern medicine.

Feedback from trusted individuals can also help you identify your "why." Ask colleagues, mentors, or friends what they perceive as your unique contributions. Often, others notice patterns in our actions that we may overlook. For example, if multiple people highlight your ability to build strong, supportive teams, this might point to a "why" centered on fostering community and collaboration.

Once you've gathered these insights, it's time to articulate your "why." A clear "why" statement ties together your values, motivations, and strengths into a concise expression of purpose. Consider Nelson Mandela's "why": a commitment to justice and equality that guided him through decades of imprisonment and political struggle. Mandela's "why" wasn't simply aspirational, it was a daily practice that shaped his choices and inspired others.

But finding your "why" is only the beginning. Purpose must be integrated into your life through intentional action. Use your "why" as a filter for decision-making. When evaluating opportunities, ask yourself: *Does this align with my purpose?* For example, if your "why" involves creativity and innovation, prioritize roles or projects that allow you to think outside the box. Similarly, if your "why" centers on making a tangible impact, look for opportunities to contribute to meaningful causes or initiatives.

Purpose also transforms how you approach routine tasks. For instance, if your "why" involves empowering others, even a mundane activity like organizing a team meeting can become an opportunity to create space for collaboration and growth. By aligning your "why" with daily actions, you infuse meaning into every aspect of your work.

Finally, recognize that your "why" evolves. Life experiences, challenges, and growth will add new dimensions to your purpose. Periodically revisit your "why" to ensure it still resonates. Consider Eleanor Roosevelt, whose "why" evolved over time from personal advocacy to a broader commitment to human rights. This adaptability allowed her to remain impactful and fulfilled throughout her life.

Finding your "why" is not just a journey of self-discovery, it's a transformative practice that shapes how you live, work, and connect with the world. From historical icons to everyday leaders, those who align their actions with their purpose create lasting impact and personal fulfillment. By discovering and living your "why," you unlock the power to navigate challenges with resilience, inspire others with authenticity, and build a life of true significance.

Chapter 6

The Zone of Genius

The Zone of Genius is not just a concept, it's a way of being, a space where your unique talents, passions, and purpose align. It's the realm where you thrive effortlessly, producing extraordinary results while feeling deeply fulfilled. Coined by Gay Hendricks in *The Big Leap*, this idea invites us to explore a life beyond competence or even excellence. It asks us to focus on what makes us come alive, what we do so naturally that it feels almost too easy, and what brings us joy while creating value for others.

To live in the Zone of Genius is to unlock a state of flow, a term popularized by psychologist Mihaly Csikszentmihalyi to describe the experience of being fully immersed in an activity. Think of a musician lost in composition, a scientist racing to capture a fleeting idea, or a teacher completely attuned to their students' needs. In these moments, time dissolves, self-doubt vanishes, and creativity soars. It's not just about doing something well, it's about doing something that feels like an extension of who you are.

The power of the Zone of Genius is rooted in both human history and modern neuroscience. Throughout time, extraordinary figures have shown us what it means to operate at the intersection of passion, talent, and purpose. Aristotle, for instance, spoke of *eudaimonia*, the idea of flourishing by living in accordance with one's true self and potential. In his view, the good life was not defined by external success but by alignment with inner virtues. This philosophy resonates with what we now understand as the Zone of Genius, a space where alignment fosters fulfillment.

Consider Leonardo da Vinci, whose genius transcended disciplines. Whether painting the *Mona Lisa* or sketching flying machines, da Vinci's brilliance lay in his ability to seamlessly integrate art, science, and imagination. His flow state was evident in the way he pursued his curiosities with relentless passion, untethered by conventional boundaries. Centuries later, another innovator, Steve Jobs, demonstrated a similar genius in his ability to blend design, technology, and user experience, reshaping entire industries through products like the iPhone. Both men lived at the cutting edge of their talents, driven by a sense of purpose that elevated their work.

What's remarkable is that this ability to operate in the Zone of Genius is not reserved for historical icons or celebrated visionaries, it is accessible to all of us. Neuroscience helps explain why this zone feels so rewarding. When you work in alignment with your natural abilities and passions, your brain's reward system releases dopamine, the chemical responsible for motivation and pleasure. This creates a positive feedback loop: the more you engage in Genius Zone activities, the more energized and fulfilled you feel, which in turn propels you to do even more. It's a self-sustaining cycle that fosters creativity, productivity, and well-being.

This effect can be seen in modern figures like Oprah Winfrey, whose Zone of Genius lies in her unparalleled ability to connect with people and facilitate transformative conversations. From her talk show to her media empire, Oprah's genius is evident not just in her success but in the authenticity of her purpose: to inspire and empower others. Her work mirrors Aristotle's notion of flourishing, combining personal fulfillment with meaningful impact.

Operating in your Zone of Genius also engages the limbic system, the emotional core of the brain. This part of the brain doesn't process language or logic but governs our feelings and instincts. It's why you can often "feel" when something resonates deeply, even if you can't immediately articulate why. Malala Yousafzai, for example, exemplifies this connection. Her advocacy for girls' education is deeply personal, driven by her lived experience and an emotional bond to her mission. Like Harriet Tubman before her, who risked everything to lead enslaved people to freedom, Malala's Zone of Genius is fueled by a profound sense of purpose that transcends fear or fatigue.

The Four Zones of Activity

Hendricks categorizes activities into four zones: Incompetence, Competence, Excellence, and Genius. Each represents a different relationship between your skills, passions, and engagement. Let's explore these in more detail.

The Zone of Incompetence

The Zone of Incompetence consists of tasks you're not good at, things that drain your energy because they don't play to your strengths. These activities often take longer than necessary and leave you feeling frustrated or inadequate. For example:

- A creative writer might struggle with creating detailed spreadsheets for project management.
- An entrepreneur who excels at vision and strategy may find themselves floundering when trying to handle IT issues.

These are tasks that others can do better, often with ease. Yet many people, out of a sense of obligation or misplaced responsibility, hold on to them. Operating in the Zone of Incompetence is a surefire way to waste time and energy while diminishing your confidence.

The solution is simple but often overlooked: *delegate.* Letting go of these tasks frees up mental and emotional bandwidth for activities that truly matter. This doesn't mean abandoning responsibility; it means recognizing that your energy is better spent elsewhere, where it can create the most value.

The Zone of Competence

The Zone of Competence includes tasks you can do adequately but that don't energize or inspire you. You're capable here, but there's nothing exceptional about your performance, and the work often feels routine or uninspiring. For example:

- A teacher may competently manage administrative paperwork but find it mundane compared to the joy of engaging with students.

- A marketing professional might be able to write ad copy but lack the enthusiasm or creative spark to make it extraordinary.

Operating in this zone often feels like going through the motions. It's easy to justify staying here because you're capable, but the cost is subtle yet significant: mediocrity. Spending too much time in the Zone of Competence leaves little room for growth or fulfillment.

The key to escaping this zone is to *automate or delegate.* If possible, use tools or systems to handle repetitive tasks, or outsource them to others who find joy and efficiency in such work. By doing so, you create space to focus on areas where you can truly shine.

The Zone of Excellence

The Zone of Excellence is where many people get stuck, and for good reason: it's a comfortable trap. This zone includes tasks you excel at, things you do better than most people. You might even enjoy them, but they don't ignite your passion or connect deeply with your purpose. They're safe, rewarding, and externally validated, which makes them hard to leave. For example:

- A corporate lawyer might excel in courtroom strategy but feel disconnected from the true impact of their work.

- A successful manager might be adept at leading teams but yearn for a more creative or entrepreneurial role.

The Zone of Excellence is seductive because it often comes with financial rewards, professional accolades, and societal approval. People in this zone are often praised for their skills and achievements, making it difficult to question whether they're truly fulfilled. It's easy to rationalize staying here: *"I'm good at this. People appreciate me. Why risk leaving?"*

But staying in the Zone of Excellence comes at a cost. It often leads to a lingering sense of dissatisfaction, a quiet, nagging feeling that something's missing. This is where cognitive dissonance sets in: your external success doesn't match your internal sense of purpose.

To move beyond the Zone of Excellence, you must ask yourself hard questions: *Am I truly passionate about this? Is this the legacy I want to leave?* Recognizing that there's more to life than external success is the first step toward breaking free.

The Zone of Genius

The Zone of Genius is where your unique talents, passions, and purpose converge. It's the space where work feels like play, where time seems to disappear, and where your contributions create the most impact. In this zone, you're not just good, you're exceptional. And it's not just about performance, it's about alignment. You're doing what you were meant to do.

People operating in their Zone of Genius often describe their work as effortless. That doesn't mean it's easy, it means it feels natural. For example:

- A writer who thrives in their Zone of Genius might lose track of time crafting a novel that feels deeply personal yet universally resonant.

- A social entrepreneur might feel energized creating innovative solutions that address systemic challenges, combining strategic thinking with a sense of mission.

What sets the Zone of Genius apart is the profound sense of fulfillment it provides. It's where your talents meet the world's needs, and the joy you derive from your work radiates outward, inspiring and benefiting others.

Living in Alignment

When you operate in your Zone of Genius, your work becomes an extension of who you are. It's not about doing everything; it's about doing the right things, the ones that light you up and leave a lasting impact. It's about escaping the inertia of competence, the comfort of excellence, and stepping into a space where your talents and passions meet the world's needs.

This isn't just about personal fulfillment, it's about creating value for others.

Identifying your Zone of Genius begins with reflection. Think about moments when you felt most alive, when time seemed to disappear, and you were fully absorbed in what you were doing. These moments often hold the key to your Genius Zone. For example, Jennifer Doudna, co-creator of CRISPR gene-editing technology, found her Genius Zone at the intersection of curiosity and problem-solving. Her work has revolutionized genetics, mirroring the groundbreaking contributions of Marie Curie, whose relentless pursuit of scientific discovery laid the foundation for modern physics and medicine. Both women demonstrate how a clear sense of genius can transform entire fields.

Feedback from others can also provide valuable insights. Sometimes, we're so close to our own strengths that we don't recognize them as unique. Ask trusted colleagues, mentors, or friends: *What do you see as my greatest strengths? When have I been at my best?* Their observations can reveal patterns you might overlook. For instance, a writer might hear repeatedly that their ability to distill complex ideas into simple, engaging narratives is a standout strength, pointing to a Zone of Genius in communication.

Once you've identified your Genius Zone, the challenge becomes living there. This requires courage, especially if it means stepping away from your Zone of Excellence, where you may be highly rewarded but unfulfilled. The key is to delegate or eliminate tasks in your Zones of Incompetence and Competence, freeing up time and energy to focus on what truly matters. For example, a leader whose Genius Zone lies in strategy might delegate operational responsibilities to concentrate on long-term vision and innovation.

Modern leaders like Elon Musk exemplify this focus. Musk's Zone of Genius lies in envisioning and executing bold ideas, from Tesla's electric vehicles to SpaceX's reusable rockets. His ability to stay centered on his genius, while building teams to handle other aspects of execution, is a major factor in his success. Similarly, historical figures like Thomas Edison operated within their Genius Zones by dedicating themselves to invention, delegating other aspects of their businesses to collaborators.

Living in your Zone of Genius isn't about achieving perfection, it's about alignment. It's about crafting a life and career where your talents, passions, and purpose intersect, creating work that feels authentic and meaningful. Whether it's Oprah inspiring millions, da Vinci bridging art and science, or an unsung hero mentoring their community, the Zone of Genius is where we all have the potential to thrive. It's a reminder that true success isn't just about what we do, it's about why and how we do it.

Part 3
The Path to Purposeful Work

From Purpose Discovery to Action

Purpose Discovery
Understanding what matters

Align Values
Integrate values into decisions

Set Intentional Goals
Establish meaningful career objectives

Navigate Transitions
Move through career changes with clarity

Infuse Meaning
Enhance current role with purpose

Purposeful Work
Fulfilling and meaningful career

Finding purpose is one thing; living it is another. The journey from discovery to action requires courage, strategy, and persistence. Purposeful work isn't just about knowing what matters to you, it's about integrating that understanding into your daily decisions, career path, and long-term goals. It's about making the transition from work that simply fills time to work that fulfills life.

This section of the book focuses on how to take the insights you've gained about your purpose and put them into practice. It's about aligning your work with your values, navigating transitions with intention, and creating a sense of meaning in the work you're doing today. Purposeful work isn't a destination, it's a practice. And like any practice, it takes effort, experimentation, and an open mind.

Over the next three chapters, we'll explore the practical steps you can take to align your career with your purpose. We'll look at how to set intentional goals that go beyond surface-level success, how to navigate career transitions with clarity and confidence, and how to infuse your current role with meaning, even if it doesn't seem purposeful at first glance. By the end of this section, you'll have the tools to build a career that reflects your values, amplifies your strengths, and contributes to the legacy you want to create.

Chapter 7

Setting Intentional Goals

Setting intentional goals is not merely about jotting down aspirations or ticking off items on a checklist. It's about aligning your actions with your purpose and using that alignment to fuel motivation, focus, and resilience. The science behind goal setting reveals its profound impact on how we think, act, and ultimately achieve. When goals resonate with our values and leverage the brain's natural processes, they become powerful catalysts for growth and transformation.

Every significant human achievement began with a clear, intentional goal. Think of the moon landing in 1969, a moment that united science, politics, and human ingenuity. The commitment to "land a man on the moon and return him safely to the Earth" wasn't just a technical challenge, it was a bold declaration that set in motion a series of actions and innovations. It inspired thousands of scientists, engineers, and astronauts to align their efforts toward a common purpose. This singular goal reshaped not just space exploration but also how humanity viewed its place in the universe.

The process of setting intentional goals is deeply embedded in how the brain functions. Neuroscientists have found that goal setting activates the brain's reward system, creating a feedback loop that reinforces behaviors aligned with those goals. Every step forward releases dopamine, the neurotransmitter responsible for feelings of pleasure and satisfaction. This is why progress feels so rewarding, it's hardwired into our biology. Imagine the joy a writer feels when completing a chapter or the exhilaration of a researcher making a breakthrough after years of effort. These moments aren't just emotional, they're chemical, driven by the brain's response to progress.

But setting a goal is only the beginning. The prefrontal cortex, the brain's center for planning and decision-making, plays a critical role in turning goals into action. This part of the brain evaluates priorities, organizes steps, and helps maintain focus in the face of distractions. For example, a vague aspiration like "get healthier" might activate a general desire, but the prefrontal cortex needs specificity to function effectively. A goal such as "exercise for 30 minutes every morning and cut sugar intake by half" provides the structure needed to drive action.

Historical examples show us the power of specificity in goal setting. During the Manhattan Project in World War II, the goal of creating an atomic bomb to end the war was both clear and urgent. Scientists like Robert Oppenheimer and Enrico Fermi didn't just work toward a vague notion of success, they were laser-focused on milestones: refining uranium, testing chain reactions, and designing delivery mechanisms. Each step was meticulously planned, and the cumulative progress led to an outcome that reshaped global politics and warfare. While the ethical implications of their work remain debated, the clarity of their goal-setting process illustrates its power.

The concept of neuroplasticity, our brain's ability to rewire itself through experience, further underscores the transformative potential of intentional goals. Each time we engage in goal-directed behavior, we strengthen the neural pathways associated with focus, creativity, and problem-solving. This adaptability is why perseverance often leads to mastery. Thomas Edison, who famously failed over a thousand times before inventing the light bulb, exemplified this principle. Each failure wasn't just a setback, it was a lesson that refined his approach and strengthened his determination. His brain, like all of ours, adapted to the challenges he faced, making each successive attempt more informed and effective.

Visualization also plays a pivotal role in goal setting. When you vividly imagine yourself achieving a goal, your brain activates many of the same regions as it does during the actual experience. This mental rehearsal primes your mind for success, creating a psychological readiness to act. Olympic athletes often use this technique, mentally practicing every move before stepping onto the field or into the pool. Michael Phelps, the most decorated Olympian of all time, credited visualization as a key component of his training, allowing him to rehearse perfect races in his mind before executing them in reality.

Intentional goals are not a modern invention, they have shaped history's most significant movements. The Civil Rights Movement in the United States, for example, was guided by clear, actionable objectives: desegregation, voting rights, and equal treatment under the law. Leaders like Martin Luther King Jr. articulated these goals with a moral clarity that inspired millions. King's "I Have a Dream" speech wasn't just a call to action, it was a vision of a world that aligned with the movement's core values. This alignment between purpose and goals created a momentum that overcame immense resistance, proving that when goals resonate deeply, they can move mountains.

In your own life, intentional goals require the same alignment. Start by identifying what truly matters to you, your "why." This foundational purpose provides the motivation needed to pursue goals even when challenges arise. Break your goals into smaller, actionable steps that allow you to track progress and celebrate milestones. Each small victory reinforces your commitment and triggers the dopamine-driven reward system, creating a cycle of positive reinforcement.

Progress may not always be linear, but even setbacks contribute to growth. Embracing obstacles as part of the journey helps reframe challenges as opportunities to adapt and learn. This mindset, rooted in neuroplasticity, allows you to approach your goals with resilience and creativity, knowing that every effort strengthens your ability to succeed.

Setting intentional goals is not just about achieving specific outcomes, it's about building a life aligned with your values and purpose. It's about creating a framework that allows you to focus your energy, harness your strengths, and navigate challenges with clarity and confidence. Whether your aspirations are personal, professional, or societal, intentional goals provide the structure needed to turn vision into reality.

The path to purposeful work begins with clarity of intent, and intentional goals are the stepping stones that make it possible to move forward with conviction and grace.

To summarize above, setting intentional goals isn't just a productivity hack, it's the cornerstone of living a life aligned with purpose. Rooted in neuroscience and validated by history's most transformative achievements, intentional goals bridge the gap between aspiration and action. They channel our energy, focus, and resilience, enabling us to turn abstract dreams into tangible outcomes. But how do you translate these concepts into actionable steps that create real change in your life? Let's explore.

Practical Steps to Build Intentional Goals (Backed by Neuroscience)

To set intentional goals that resonate deeply and drive meaningful action, it's essential to ground the process in evidence-based practices. Here's how to do it:

1. **Anchor Your Goals in Personal Values**

    - **Neuroscience Insight**: The limbic system, the brain's emotional center, processes decisions rooted in values more deeply than those driven by external motivations. Goals aligned with personal values create stronger emotional engagement, increasing motivation and resilience.

    - **Action**: Reflect on what truly matters to you. Write down your top five core values, whether it's creativity, freedom, family, or growth, and ensure your goals align with these priorities.

    - **Example**: Instead of setting a generic goal like "Get promoted," frame it as "Earn a leadership role that allows me to mentor others and foster innovation," if those values resonate with you.

2. **Make Goals Specific and Actionable**

    - **Neuroscience Insight**: The prefrontal cortex thrives on specificity. Vague goals overstimulate this part of the brain, leading to decision fatigue and decreased focus. Specific goals provide a clear roadmap, reducing cognitive load.

    - **Action**: Avoid ambiguous statements like "Improve my fitness." Instead, break it into actionable steps, such as "Run three times a week for 30 minutes and eat two servings of vegetables daily."

- **Example**: If your goal is financial security, specify actions like "Save $500 each month by automating deposits into a high-yield savings account."

3. **Visualize Success Regularly**

   - **Neuroscience Insight**: Mental imagery activates brain regions associated with actual task performance, such as the motor and sensory cortices. This primes the brain for action and reinforces commitment.

   - **Action**: Spend 5-10 minutes daily visualizing yourself achieving your goal. Picture the details, the environment, your emotions, and the results.

   - **Example**: If you're preparing for a public speech, imagine standing confidently before the audience, delivering your message with clarity and poise, and receiving applause.

4. **Break Goals into Manageable Milestones**

   - **Neuroscience Insight**: Dopamine is released when progress is made, reinforcing goal-directed behavior. Breaking large goals into smaller milestones ensures consistent dopamine-driven motivation.

   - **Action**: Divide your goal into phases or steps. Celebrate each milestone to maintain momentum.

   - **Example**: Writing a book? Break it down into "Outline chapters," "Write 1,000 words per week," and "Complete a draft in six months."

5. **Set Deadlines to Create Urgency**
    - **Neuroscience Insight**: Time-bound goals activate the prefrontal cortex's ability to prioritize and manage resources. Deadlines create a sense of urgency that enhances focus.
    - **Action**: Attach specific dates to your milestones. Use tools like calendars or apps to track your progress and hold yourself accountable.
    - **Example**: "Complete my portfolio by October 31" is more actionable than "Work on my portfolio."

6. **Incorporate Feedback Loops**
    - **Neuroscience Insight**: Constructive feedback triggers dopamine release, reinforcing learning and adaptation. It also helps refine neural pathways associated with goal achievement.
    - **Action**: Seek regular feedback from mentors, peers, or trusted friends. Use their insights to adjust your approach without losing sight of the larger goal.
    - **Example**: If you're building a business, share your progress with a mentor monthly and incorporate their suggestions into your strategy.

7. **Cultivate a Growth Mindset**
    - **Neuroscience Insight**: Neuroplasticity ensures that challenges strengthen the brain's problem-solving circuits. Viewing obstacles as opportunities rewires the brain for resilience.

- **Action**: Reframe setbacks as learning experiences. Ask yourself, "What can I learn from this challenge?" And apply those lessons moving forward.

- **Example**: If a job application is rejected, use it as a chance to refine your resume and prepare more thoroughly for the next opportunity.

8. **Track Progress and Celebrate Wins**

    - **Neuroscience Insight**: Tracking progress and celebrating achievements trigger dopamine release, reinforcing the behaviors that led to success. This creates a positive feedback loop for continued effort.

    - **Action**: Use journals, apps, or charts to monitor your progress. Celebrate small victories, whether it's a dinner out, a relaxing day off, or sharing your success with friends.

    - **Example**: After completing a major work project, reward yourself with something meaningful, a weekend trip or a new book.

By incorporating these steps, you align your actions with your purpose, activate your brain's natural mechanisms for focus and motivation, and set yourself up for success. These aren't just theoretical strategies, they are tools for building intentionality into your life and work.

Chapter 8

Purposeful Transitions

Transitions in life are inevitable. They mark the spaces between one chapter and the next, moments of change that can feel unsettling yet hold immense potential. Purposeful transitions, however, are different. They aren't just about moving forward, they're about moving forward with clarity, intention, and alignment. These transitions require a deep understanding of what truly matters to you and a willingness to reshape your path to reflect those values. From career changes to life shifts, transitions grounded in purpose have the power to unlock fulfillment and growth.

Purposeful transitions are deeply connected to how our brains work. Neuroscience reveals that the brain is built for adaptation; it thrives on change when that change is intentional. At the heart of this adaptability lies neuroplasticity, the brain's ability to rewire itself in response to new experiences. When you embrace a purposeful transition, whether it's pursuing a new career, shifting your priorities, or redefining your goals, you engage this remarkable capacity for growth. Each step forward strengthens neural pathways, making it easier to navigate future changes. Purpose becomes the compass that guides this process, turning what might otherwise feel chaotic into a deliberate, meaningful journey.

Throughout history, transitions have played a pivotal role in shaping not only individual lives but entire societies. Think of the Agricultural Revolution, when humanity shifted from nomadic hunting and gathering to settled farming communities. This wasn't just a practical adjustment, it was a profound transformation of how people lived, worked, and connected. Similarly, the Industrial Revolution upended traditional ways of life, forcing individuals to leave rural farms for urban factories. These transitions were often disruptive, but they also paved the way for progress. The same is true on a personal level: while transitions can be uncomfortable, they hold the potential for profound growth when approached with intention.

On an individual scale, purposeful transitions can look like stepping away from a comfortable career to pursue a passion or redefining your identity in retirement after decades of professional life. Consider the experience of Viktor Frankl, a Holocaust survivor and renowned psychologist. Frankl's ability to find meaning in even the most harrowing circumstances reshaped his purpose and led to his groundbreaking work in logotherapy. He demonstrated that transitions, no matter how challenging, can be opportunities to realign with what matters most.

Purposeful transitions are also fueled by the brain's reward system. When you set goals that align with your values, the neurotransmitter dopamine is released, creating a sense of motivation and pleasure. This is why small steps, like learning a new skill or making progress toward a meaningful goal, feel so rewarding. The brain reinforces these actions, creating a positive feedback loop that drives further growth. This process is especially powerful during transitions, when clarity and intentionality are crucial for navigating uncertainty.

Transitions often require heightened cognitive effort, engaging the prefrontal cortex, the part of the brain responsible for decision-making, planning, and self-regulation. This region evaluates options, anticipates outcomes, and helps you make choices that align with your long-term vision. To support this process, practices like mindfulness and journaling can enhance clarity and focus, allowing you to approach transitions with greater confidence.

History is full of examples of individuals and movements that embraced purposeful transitions to create lasting impact. Martin Luther King Jr. led the Civil Rights Movement through one of the most profound societal transitions in modern history, advocating for equality with unwavering clarity and purpose. His leadership demonstrates how aligning actions with deeply held values can transform not only individual lives but entire systems. On a personal level, consider the story of Malala Yousafzai, who transitioned from a young girl advocating for her education to a global icon for women's rights. Her journey reflects the power of purpose to guide transitions, even in the face of immense adversity.

But how do we translate these lessons into our own lives? Purposeful transitions require intentional steps. First, self-reflection is essential. You must understand what drives you, what fulfills you, and what you want to contribute to the world. This clarity serves as a foundation for all decisions moving forward. Next, breaking larger transitions into smaller, actionable steps can make the process more manageable. Each small step not only builds momentum but also reinforces the neural pathways associated with growth and resilience.

Visualization is another powerful too

l. By imagining yourself thriving in your new chapter, whether it's starting a new job, moving to a new city, or embracing a new role, you prepare your brain for success. This mental rehearsal creates a sense of familiarity and confidence, making the transition feel less daunting.

Support systems are equally important. Surrounding yourself with mentors, peers, or loved ones who understand and support your goals can provide invaluable encouragement and perspective. Their insights can help you navigate challenges and celebrate progress, reminding you that you're not alone in your journey.

Transitions also require patience and self-compassion. They often come with setbacks, moments of doubt, and unexpected challenges. But these obstacles are part of the process. They provide opportunities to adapt, learn, and grow. A growth mindset, the belief that abilities can be developed through effort and persistence, can make all the difference. Each challenge you overcome strengthens your capacity to navigate future transitions with confidence.

In the end, purposeful transitions are about alignment. They're about ensuring that your actions, decisions, and aspirations reflect who you truly are and what you value most. They're not just moments of change, they're opportunities to become more fully yourself. Whether you're stepping into a new role, redefining your priorities, or charting an entirely new path, transitions guided by purpose are transformative. They allow you to move forward with clarity, confidence, and a deep sense of fulfillment, knowing that each step is taking you closer to the life you're meant to lead.

Following through purposeful transitions requires more than intention, it demands actionable steps that align your thoughts, behaviors, and goals. Here's how to move closer to your purpose while making the process manageable and meaningful:

1. **Engage in Deep Self-Reflection**
    - *Action*: Dedicate time to understand your core values, passions, and aspirations. Journaling, meditation, or long walks can provide clarity. Ask yourself questions like:
        - What truly matters to me?
        - What would I do if I weren't afraid of failing?
        - What legacy do I want to leave behind?
    - *Why it works*: Reflection engages the prefrontal cortex, enhancing your ability to evaluate options and align decisions with long-term goals.

2. **Identify Specific Areas for Change**
    - *Action*: Pinpoint the aspects of your life or career that feel misaligned with your purpose. Be honest about what drains your energy versus what excites you.
        - For example, if your current job feels unfulfilling, identify whether it's the work itself, the environment, or the lack of growth opportunities.
    - *Why it works*: This targeted analysis helps you focus on actionable solutions rather than feeling overwhelmed by the scope of the transition.

3. **Visualize the Desired Outcome**
    - *Action*: Create a vivid mental image of your life after the transition. Picture the details: where you are, what you're doing, how it feels.

- o For instance, if you're transitioning to a new career, imagine yourself thriving in the role, your workplace, your colleagues, and your impact.
- *Why it works*: Visualization activates the brain's reward system, priming it for success and reducing the fear of the unknown.

4. **Break Down the Transition into Manageable Steps**
   - *Action*: Divide your transition into smaller, actionable goals. For example:
     - o Update your resume or portfolio.
     - o Schedule informational interviews with people in your desired field.
     - o Enroll in a course to develop new skills.
   - *Why it works*: Breaking transitions into steps creates a sense of progress, triggering dopamine release and reinforcing your commitment.

5. **Seek Guidance and Build Support Networks**
   - *Action*: Surround yourself with mentors, peers, and trusted advisors who can offer guidance and encouragement.
     - o Join professional groups or communities aligned with your goals.
     - o Share your intentions with close friends or family for accountability.
   - *Why it works*: Support systems provide valuable perspectives, reduce feelings of isolation, and bolster your resilience during challenging moments.

6. **Leverage Neuroplasticity by Learning and Adapting**
    - *Action*: Embrace new challenges as opportunities to grow. Take on projects, roles, or responsibilities that stretch your skills and align with your aspirations.
        o For example, if you're transitioning into entrepreneurship, start by managing a small-scale project to build confidence and skills.
    - *Why it works*: Engaging in new experiences strengthens neural pathways, making future transitions easier and more effective.

7. **Develop Resilience Through Mindfulness Practices**
    - *Action*: Incorporate mindfulness techniques like meditation, breathing exercises, or reflective journaling into your routine. These practices enhance clarity and reduce stress during transitions.
    - *Why it works*: Mindfulness strengthens the prefrontal cortex, improving decision-making and emotional regulation when facing uncertainty.

8. **Track Progress and Celebrate Wins**
    - *Action*: Regularly review your progress. Create a visual tracker, such as a chart or list, to mark completed milestones. Celebrate even small victories, like sending an email to a mentor or completing a training module.
    - *Why it works*: Tracking progress reinforces positive behaviors, while celebrating wins triggers dopamine release, motivating you to keep moving forward.

9. **Reframe Setbacks as Learning Opportunities**

    - *Action*: When challenges arise, pause to reflect on what they can teach you. Reframe failures as steps in the learning process. Ask yourself:

        o What can I learn from this?

        o How can I adapt my approach to move forward?

    - *Why it works*: A growth mindset rewires the brain to view challenges as opportunities, fostering resilience and creativity.

10. **Revisit and Refine Your Purpose Regularly**

    - *Action*: Schedule regular check-ins with yourself to assess whether your actions still align with your values and purpose. Adjust your goals and strategies as needed.

    - *Why it works*: Purpose evolves over time. Staying attuned to these changes ensures that your transitions remain aligned with what truly matters.

11. **Take the First Step Without Overthinking**

    - *Action*: Begin immediately with one small, purposeful action. Whether it's sending an email, enrolling in a course, or updating your resume, taking the first step creates momentum.

    - *Why it works*: Starting breaks the inertia of indecision and sets the transition in motion, building confidence through action.

12. **Stay Patient and Trust the Process**

- *Action*: Accept that purposeful transitions take time. Focus on consistency rather than immediate results. Celebrate the journey as much as the destination.

- *Why it works*: Patience reinforces emotional resilience, helping you stay committed even when progress feels slow.

Purposeful transitions are not merely moments of change, they are opportunities to redefine your life, your values, and your impact on the world. They invite you to step into the discomfort of the unknown with clarity and intention, to let go of what no longer serves you, and to embrace a future aligned with your true self.

Transitions, by their nature, are messy. They can be fraught with uncertainty, fear, and self-doubt. But they are also the fertile ground where growth begins. They are the spaces between what was and what could be, the moments when we're forced to reckon with who we are and what we want to become. They demand courage, but they also reward us with a life of greater alignment, purpose, and fulfillment.

Through the lens of neuroscience, we see how our brains are designed to adapt and thrive when we approach change with intention. History shows us that purposeful transitions have the power to shape not only individual lives but entire societies. And through personal reflection, deliberate action, and resilience, we can navigate even the most challenging transitions with grace.

As you embark on your own transitions, remember that this process is not about perfection; it's about progress. It's about taking small, meaningful steps toward the life you envision, celebrating the milestones along the way, and learning from the setbacks. It's about trusting that each decision, each action, is bringing you closer to a life that truly reflects your values and aspirations.

Every purposeful transition begins with a choice: to move forward, to grow, and to align your life with what truly matters. The path won't always be easy, but it will always be worth it. Because in the end, purposeful transitions are not just about what you gain, they are about who you become.

Chapter 9

Building Meaning into Your Work Today

Work is more than just a means of earning a living, it can be a profound source of fulfillment, creativity, and connection when imbued with meaning. Building meaning into your work requires a shift in perspective, an understanding of how our brains process purpose, and a commitment to aligning your daily actions with your values. While it may sound abstract, the process is grounded in evidence-based neuroscience, psychological frameworks, and real-world examples that demonstrate how even small changes can lead to transformative outcomes.

The Neuroscience of Meaningful Work

The human brain is wired to seek meaning and purpose. Neuroscientific research has uncovered several key mechanisms that explain how work becomes meaningful and why this matters.

1. **The Role of the Default Mode Network (DMN):** The DMN, a network of brain regions active during rest and self-referential thinking, plays a central role in how we perceive meaning. This network is engaged when we reflect on our values, aspirations, and how our actions align with our sense of self.

- **Evidence**: Studies have shown that engaging the DMN through mindfulness or journaling enhances self-awareness and emotional regulation, allowing individuals to connect their tasks to larger goals.

- **Practical Insight**: Build regular reflection into your routine. For example, spend five minutes each morning contemplating how your work contributes to your personal mission or the broader impact you want to create.

2. **Neurotransmitters and Emotional Resonance**: Dopamine, serotonin, and oxytocin, three key neurotransmitters, shape our emotional responses to work. Dopamine drives motivation, serotonin regulates mood, and oxytocin fosters trust and connection.

    - **Evidence**: Research published in the *Journal of Neuroscience* highlights that positive workplace interactions and a sense of achievement trigger these neurotransmitters, creating a feedback loop of motivation and well-being.

    - **Practical Insight**: Foster these responses by setting achievable milestones (dopamine), expressing gratitude to colleagues (oxytocin), and aligning tasks with personal values (serotonin).

3. **Cognitive Dissonance and Misalignment**: Cognitive dissonance occurs when there is a conflict between actions and values, leading to discomfort and disengagement. For example, someone who values creativity but spends most of their workday on repetitive, unchallenging tasks may feel a sense of inner conflict.

- **Evidence**: A study by the American Psychological Association found that individuals who perceive their work as misaligned with their values are more likely to experience stress, burnout, and reduced productivity.

- **Practical Insight**: Conduct a values assessment to identify misalignments. For example, if you value innovation, seek opportunities to work on projects that allow for creative problem-solving, even within a larger role.

The Psychological Framework of Meaning

Psychological theories also shed light on how to create meaningful work experiences. Viktor Frankl's logotherapy, for instance, emphasizes the importance of finding meaning even in challenging circumstances. Frankl's belief that purpose can transform suffering into growth provides a valuable lens for reframing how we approach difficult tasks.

Evidence from Modern Psychology

- A study published in *Psychological Science* found that individuals with a clear sense of purpose are more resilient to stress and perform better in high-pressure environments. This resilience stems from having a "north star" that guides decisions and actions.

- Applying this concept, finding meaning in work involves reframing challenges as opportunities to grow, aligning tasks with broader goals, and actively seeking ways to contribute beyond immediate responsibilities.

Practical Strategies for Building Meaning into Work

Here's how to apply these insights in your daily life, backed by evidence and actionable steps.

1. **Craft a Personal Mission Statement**
   - **Evidence**: Research by Gallup found that employees who can articulate how their work aligns with their values report higher job satisfaction and productivity.
   - **Action**: Reflect on your core values and passions. Write a statement that encapsulates your purpose in life and how your work fits into that vision. For example, "I aim to use my problem-solving skills to make processes more efficient and create value for others." Display this statement prominently to remind yourself of your purpose.

2. **Reframe Tasks Through Reflection**
   - **Evidence**: Studies on cognitive reframing show that shifting perspectives on mundane tasks increases engagement and reduces burnout.
   - **Action**: Instead of seeing a repetitive task as a chore, connect it to its larger impact. For example, if you're managing data, consider how accurate records contribute to the success of your team or organization.

3. **Incorporate Purposeful Pauses**
   - **Evidence**: Research from the *Journal of Occupational Health Psychology* found that intentional breaks

improve focus and satisfaction by reconnecting individuals to their goals.

- **Action**: Use the Pomodoro Technique (25 minutes of focused work followed by a 5-minute reflective break) to think about how each task aligns with your values.

4. **Foster Gratitude and Connection**
    - **Evidence**: A study from the *Greater Good Science Center* at UC Berkeley found that workplaces with strong cultures of gratitude and connection report higher levels of employee engagement and well-being.
    - **Action**: Start or end your day by expressing gratitude to a colleague or team member. Simple acts like thanking someone for their support or recognizing their contributions create emotional bonds that enhance work meaning.

5. **Connect Work to Broader Societal Impact**
    - **Evidence**: The Edelman Trust Barometer found that employees who see their work contributing to societal good are more engaged and motivated.
    - **Action**: Look for ways your role impacts the community or larger industry. For instance, if you work in marketing, consider how your campaigns influence public awareness of important issues.

6. **Create Daily Reflection Rituals**
    - **Evidence**: Research published in *Frontiers in Psychology* highlights that reflection enhances self-awareness and aligns actions with values.
    - **Action**: Spend 5-10 minutes each evening reflecting on what you accomplished, how it aligns with your mission, and what you learned. Over time, this ritual reinforces purpose and progress.

7. **Set Growth-Oriented Goals**
    - **Evidence**: Carol Dweck's research on the growth mindset shows that viewing challenges as opportunities fosters resilience and meaning.
    - **Action**: Identify areas for growth and set specific goals, such as learning a new skill or taking on a stretch project, to build your capabilities and sense of accomplishment.

8. **Seek Alignment and Adjustments**
    - **Evidence**: Studies on job crafting suggest that small adjustments to roles can significantly enhance meaning and engagement.
    - **Action**: Identify areas where your strengths and passions align with your responsibilities. Propose adjustments to your role or take on projects that better align with your purpose.

It's also important to recognize that building meaning into work is not a linear process. There will be days when the "why" feels elusive, when tasks seem overwhelming, or when progress feels slow. These moments are opportunities to pause, reflect, and recalibrate. Even the smallest steps, expressing gratitude to a colleague, celebrating a completed task, or revisiting your personal mission, can reignite a sense of purpose. Meaning is not a fixed destination; it's something we cultivate daily.

By weaving intentionality into your work, you're not just improving your job satisfaction, you're laying the foundation for a life that feels aligned and fulfilling. Every decision, every task, every interaction becomes an opportunity to reinforce your sense of purpose. And when the day ends, you'll find yourself looking back not with a sense of exhaustion but with the quiet satisfaction of knowing that your work truly mattered.

Part 4
The Toolkit for Intentionality

Journey to Intentional Living

Recognize Distractions

Understand Intentionality

Develop Awareness

Design Supportive Environment

Sustain Intentionality

Intentionality is not a destination, nor is it a fleeting moment of clarity. It is a daily practice, a disciplined way of navigating life that demands focus, self-awareness, and an unrelenting commitment to aligning actions with values. It is the foundation upon which meaningful lives are built, the force that transforms scattered ambitions into purposeful progress. While earlier parts of this book delved into the importance of purpose and the challenges of finding alignment, this section is about equipping you with the tools to live intentionally, every single day.

Life is full of distractions, choices, and unexpected detours. Without a clear framework, it's easy to lose sight of what truly matters, to be pulled in directions that don't serve your aspirations, or to find yourself simply going through the motions. Intentionality, however, demands a different approach, a deliberate way of living that ensures every decision, every action, contributes to your larger purpose. It isn't about perfection or rigid control, but about cultivating awareness and making choices that reflect your values and aspirations.

This toolkit is designed to help you bridge the gap between knowing your purpose and living it. Grounded in neuroscience, psychology, and practical application, these tools provide a structured yet flexible roadmap for creating a life of alignment. They will teach you how to pause and reflect, to recognize patterns that don't serve you, and to replace them with habits and systems that support your growth. You will learn how to design your environment, your time, and even your mindset in ways that reinforce your intentional goals. Most importantly, this section will show you how to sustain intentionality even in the face of resistance, setbacks, and doubt.

Intentionality isn't about striving to control every aspect of life; it's about learning to respond to life with clarity and purpose. It's about becoming the architect of your own journey, creating a life that feels deeply fulfilling and uniquely your own. With these tools in hand, you'll be better equipped to navigate challenges, seize opportunities, and align every facet of your life with the values and aspirations that matter most to you.

Chapter 10

The Power of Reflection

Reflection is a gateway to self-awareness, growth, and alignment. It allows us to step back from the noise of daily life, examine our experiences, and extract valuable insights that shape our future. In a world that glorifies busyness, reflection offers a rare opportunity to pause, think, and reconnect with our deeper intentions. Far from being a passive process, it is an active, transformative practice that enhances decision-making, fosters emotional resilience, and empowers us to live and work with greater purpose.

At the heart of reflection lies the brain's natural capacity for introspection and learning. Neuroscience reveals that engaging in reflective practices activates key areas of the brain, such as the **Default Mode Network (DMN)**, which is responsible for self-referential thought. This network helps us draw connections between past experiences and future possibilities, providing the clarity needed to align our actions with our values. Similarly, the **prefrontal cortex**, which governs decision-making and planning, becomes more active during reflection, enabling us to analyze our thoughts critically and make more informed choices. The **hippocampus**, the brain's memory center, facilitates the recall of past events, helping us learn from both successes and failures. Together, these brain regions create a powerful foundation for personal and professional growth.

Reflection is not just a mental exercise; it has tangible emotional benefits. By engaging with our emotions in a deliberate way, we regulate stress and develop greater emotional intelligence. Research shows that reflecting on emotional responses enhances resilience, allowing us to approach challenges with a calmer, more balanced perspective. For example, leaders who regularly reflect on their decision-making processes are better equipped to manage crises, adapt to change, and build trust within their teams.

This is not a new idea. David Kolb's **Experiential Learning Theory** emphasizes the importance of reflecting on experiences as a critical step in learning and growth. Kolb's model suggests that effective learning involves a cycle of concrete experiences, reflective observation, abstract conceptualization, and active experimentation. Reflection is the bridge between experience and action, transforming raw events into meaningful lessons that guide future behavior. Similarly, the **GROW Model**, a widely used coaching framework, places reflection at its core by encouraging individuals to assess their current realities before exploring options and committing to action.

But how do we translate the concept of reflection into daily practice? The tools and methods available are as diverse as the benefits they offer. One of the most accessible methods is **journaling**. Writing about daily experiences, emotions, and insights creates a tangible record of your thoughts, making it easier to identify patterns and track growth. Journals can be tailored to specific goals, such as gratitude journals that cultivate a positive mindset or reflective journals that delve into lessons learned from challenges. The act of writing itself enhances clarity and focus, reinforcing neural pathways associated with self-awareness.

Another effective tool is **guided reflection questions**. Questions like "What did I achieve today?" "What challenges did I face, and how did I respond?" or "How do my actions align with my core values?" serve as prompts to deepen your understanding of your thoughts and behaviors. These questions encourage critical thinking and help uncover areas for improvement or alignment.

For those who prefer visual methods, **mind mapping** can be a powerful technique. By organizing thoughts visually, mind maps reveal connections between ideas that might not be immediately obvious. They're particularly useful for exploring complex issues, brainstorming solutions, or planning next steps in a reflective process.

Reflection doesn't have to be a solitary activity. **Peer reflection sessions** provide an opportunity to gain new perspectives by discussing experiences with colleagues, mentors, or friends. These sessions often uncover blind spots and foster collaborative learning, enriching the reflective process. Whether it's a formal debrief after a project or an informal conversation over coffee, engaging with others can amplify the insights gained through reflection.

For those seeking a quieter, more introspective approach, **mindfulness practices** like meditation or focused breathing are invaluable. These practices encourage present-moment awareness, creating the mental space needed for deep reflection. Neuroscientific studies show that mindfulness enhances prefrontal cortex function, improving decision-making and emotional regulation during reflective practices.

Reflection is particularly powerful in the context of work and career. In business settings, it can enhance decision-making by allowing leaders to analyze past choices and their outcomes critically. Organizations that foster a culture of reflection report greater innovation and problem-solving abilities among their teams. Employees who regularly reflect on their roles and contributions are more likely to identify areas for growth, adapt to changes, and align their work with organizational goals.

Take, for example, the story of Howard Schultz, the former CEO of Starbucks. Schultz often spoke about his practice of reflecting on the company's mission and his personal leadership philosophy. This habit enabled him to navigate the company through major transitions, including its global expansion and strategic restructuring. His reflections on purpose and impact helped maintain Starbucks' cultural values even as the business evolved, demonstrating how intentional reflection can drive success on both personal and organizational levels.

Reflection is not about dwelling on the past; it's about learning from it. By engaging in deliberate, consistent reflection, you create a feedback loop that strengthens your ability to adapt, grow, and make intentional choices. It's a practice that builds self-awareness and fosters alignment, allowing you to approach life and work with a clearer sense of direction. The tools for reflection, journaling, guided questions, mind mapping, peer sessions, and mindfulness, are not just techniques; they are doorways to transformation. They help you pause and recalibrate, ensuring that your actions reflect your values and aspirations. By incorporating these practices into your daily routine, you can harness the power of reflection to live with greater intentionality, resilience, and fulfillment.

Practices and Methods to Deepen Reflection

Effective reflection doesn't happen by accident, it requires intention and the use of evidence-based practices. Here are methods to enhance your reflective process, supported by scientific insights and real-world applications.

1. **Journaling: Writing for Clarity:** Journaling is one of the most accessible and impactful tools for reflection. Writing activates multiple cognitive functions, helping to organize thoughts, process emotions, and uncover patterns. Studies published in the *Journal of Psychology* show that individuals who journal regularly experience increased self-awareness and reduced stress levels.

   - **Gratitude Journals**: Focus on positive experiences and what you're thankful for. This practice shifts your mindset toward optimism and fosters emotional resilience.

   - **Reflective Journals**: Write about daily events, decisions, and emotions. For example, note what went well, what didn't, and what you learned. Over time, this creates a record of growth and insights.

   - **Practice**: Dedicate 10-15 minutes daily to journaling. Use prompts like:
     - *What did I learn today?*
     - *What could I have done differently?*
     - *How does today's experience align with my values?*

2. **Guided Reflection Questions: Structured Introspection:** Asking the right questions can unlock deeper insights and steer reflection in meaningful directions. Questions act as prompts to focus your thoughts and encourage critical analysis.

- **Examples**:
  - *What challenges did I face this week, and how did I handle them?*
  - *What tasks felt most meaningful, and why?*
  - *How do my recent decisions align with my long-term goals?*
- **Evidence**: Research from Harvard Business Review indicates that managers who used guided reflection questions improved their decision-making and leadership effectiveness.
- **Practice**: Set aside time each week to answer reflective questions in a journal or discussion with a mentor.

3. **Mind Mapping: Visualizing Insights:** Mind mapping transforms abstract thoughts into clear, visual connections. By creating a diagram of your reflections, you can see relationships between ideas, identify recurring themes, and prioritize actions.

   - **How to Use**: Start with a central theme (e.g., "Career Growth") and branch out with subcategories like "Strengths," "Challenges," and "Opportunities." Add specific experiences or insights under each branch.
   - **Evidence**: Studies from the *Journal of Cognitive Psychology* show that visual representation enhances memory retention and problem-solving abilities.
   - **Practice**: Use a digital tool like MindMeister or traditional pen and paper to map out your thoughts after key events or milestones.

4. **Peer Reflection: Learning Through Dialogue:** Discussing experiences with trusted peers or mentors provides new perspectives and helps identify blind spots. These conversations encourage collaborative learning and challenge assumptions.

    - **How to Use**: Schedule regular reflection sessions with a colleague or mentor. Share your experiences and ask for feedback on decisions or behaviors.

    - **Evidence**: A study by Stanford University found that peer reflection improved participants' ability to set and achieve meaningful goals.

    - **Practice**: Create a monthly routine of one-on-one discussions with a trusted advisor or participate in group reflection workshops.

5. **Meditation and Mindfulness: Enhancing Present-Moment Awareness:** Mindfulness practices help create the mental clarity needed for effective reflection. Techniques like meditation or focused breathing reduce stress and improve focus, making it easier to analyze experiences objectively.

    - **How to Use**: Dedicate 5-10 minutes daily to mindfulness exercises. Focus on your breath, observe your thoughts without judgment, and identify recurring themes or emotions.

    - **Evidence**: Neuroscientific research shows that mindfulness increases activity in the prefrontal cortex, enhancing self-awareness and decision-making.

- **Practice**: Start your day with a brief meditation, reflecting on your intentions and goals.

6. **Reflection Rituals: Daily Practices for Consistency:** Rituals anchor reflection in your routine, ensuring it becomes a consistent habit rather than an occasional activity. These rituals provide a structured way to evaluate progress and set intentions.

- **Examples**:
    o Morning Ritual: Spend 5 minutes visualizing your day and its alignment with your purpose.
    o Evening Ritual: Write down one achievement, one lesson, and one area for improvement.
- **Evidence**: Research from the *University of Southern California* shows that reflective rituals improve emotional regulation and long-term goal achievement.

How Reflection Impacts Career and Business

Reflection is not just a personal tool, it has profound implications for professional success. In the workplace, reflective practices enhance decision-making, foster continuous learning, and build emotional intelligence. Leaders who reflect on their decisions and behaviors create more inclusive, innovative, and effective teams. Organizations that encourage employee reflection see improvements in problem-solving, collaboration, and adaptability.

Take the example of Satya Nadella, CEO of Microsoft, who emphasizes the importance of a "learn-it-all" culture over a "know-it-all" mindset. Nadella's approach to reflective leadership transformed Microsoft's organizational culture, fostering collaboration and innovation. By encouraging employees to reflect on their goals and align them with the company's mission, Nadella demonstrated how reflection drives both personal and collective success.

Practical Steps to Deepen Reflection

1. **Establish a Reflection Routine**: Choose a specific time each day or week for reflective practices, such as journaling or meditation.

2. **Use Prompts and Questions**: Start with structured prompts to guide your thoughts. Over time, adapt these to focus on specific goals or challenges.

3. **Leverage Technology**: Use digital tools like journaling apps (Day One, Notion) or mind-mapping software to organize your reflections.

4. **Seek External Feedback**: Incorporate peer discussions or mentoring sessions into your reflective routine to gain new perspectives.

5. **Celebrate Progress**: Regularly review past reflections to see how far you've come and reinforce positive behaviors.

Reflection is more than looking back, it's about moving forward with clarity and purpose. By engaging in deliberate practices like journaling, guided questions, and mindfulness, you can harness the power of reflection to make better decisions, build emotional resilience, and create a life aligned with your values. Every reflective moment is an investment in growth, ensuring that your actions are not just productive but meaningful.

Chapter 11

Designing Your Purpose Ecosystem

Imagine walking into a room where everything feels right, your tools are within reach, the light is perfect, the air is just the right temperature, and you're surrounded by people who inspire you. That's what living in a purpose ecosystem feels like, but on a much grander scale. It's not just about having a physical workspace that supports your productivity; it's about creating an interconnected framework in your life where every element, your environment, relationships, goals, and mindset, aligns to support your purpose.

Designing this ecosystem is not just a nice-to-have; it's essential for thriving in both your personal and professional life. Without it, even the most well-intentioned goals can feel like a slog, and the most inspirational ideas can lose their spark. This chapter builds on everything we've explored so far, tying together the power of reflection, intentionality, and purpose into a system you can rely on daily. Historical examples, evidence-based practices, and modern neuroscience all converge here to show us how to build and sustain this ecosystem.

The Interplay of Systems: Learning from the Past

Urie Bronfenbrenner's **Ecological Systems Theory** offers a powerful lens to understand how our lives are shaped by layers of influence. At its heart, the theory highlights that our development, and by extension, our ability to live with purpose, is influenced by the interplay of four systems:

1. **Microsystem**: Think of this as your immediate environment, your workplace, your closest relationships, and your day-to-day activities. In business history, we see this reflected in the culture of organizations like Apple under Steve Jobs. Jobs fostered an environment where innovation was the norm and creativity was celebrated, aligning the microsystem of Apple employees with the company's larger vision.

2. **Mesosystem**: This is where different parts of your life connect. For example, how does your family life affect your work, or how does your social circle influence your career decisions? Consider Andrew Carnegie, who built his steel empire while cultivating relationships that aligned with his philanthropic goals, bridging personal ambition with societal impact.

3. **Exosystem**: External factors like industry trends, government policies, or market conditions. Take the rise of Corporate Social Responsibility (CSR) in the late 20th century, companies like Ben & Jerry's thrived by integrating environmental and social concerns into their business strategy, aligning external pressures with internal purpose.

4. **Macrosystem**: The broader societal and cultural context. During the Industrial Revolution, Henry Ford revolutionized manufacturing with the assembly line, aligning his work with the societal need for affordable transportation, thereby embedding purpose within a larger cultural shift.

Understanding these layers helps you identify where alignment exists, and where it doesn't. For example, if your workplace values conflict with your personal principles, that misalignment can create friction that undermines your purpose ecosystem.

Fueling Purpose: The Science of Motivation

Living a purpose-driven life also requires that your ecosystem satisfies the fundamental psychological needs outlined in Edward Deci and Richard Ryan's **Self-Determination Theory**: autonomy, competence, and relatedness. These needs are essential not just for personal fulfillment but for driving meaningful work.

- **Autonomy**: This is the freedom to make decisions and chart your path. Google's famous "20% Time," which allowed employees to dedicate a fifth of their work hours to passion projects, led to innovations like Gmail. Autonomy fosters creativity and alignment with personal purpose.

- **Competence**: Mastery of your craft is equally critical. During World War II, the Manhattan Project brought together the world's brightest minds in physics. The immense challenges pushed these individuals to their limits, fostering a deep sense of purpose through competence and achievement.

- **Relatedness**: The connections you cultivate can amplify your sense of purpose. Patagonia exemplifies this principle by fostering a culture of environmental stewardship, creating bonds between employees and a shared mission to protect the planet.

To build a purpose ecosystem, focus on roles, projects, and environments that satisfy these needs. Whether it's choosing work that challenges you to grow (competence) or surrounding yourself with like-minded collaborators (relatedness), every decision shapes the ecosystem.

Building Resilience: Lessons from a Growth Mindset

Carol Dweck's **Growth Mindset** teaches us that purpose ecosystems thrive when they embrace challenges and failures as opportunities for growth. Consider Thomas Edison, who famously reframed thousands of failed experiments as steps toward discovering the lightbulb. His growth mindset allowed him to persist and innovate, exemplifying how resilience can fuel purpose.

In your own ecosystem, this means:

- Seeing challenges as experiments. If a new role or project doesn't go as planned, analyze what you learned and adjust.

- Surrounding yourself with people who encourage growth. Seek out mentors or peers who challenge you constructively and inspire you to improve.

Connecting the Dots: Systems Thinking in Action

Designing a purpose ecosystem also requires a holistic perspective. **Systems Thinking** helps us see how various parts of our lives, work, relationships, health, interconnect. By understanding these interactions, you can create a life where every element reinforces the others.

- **Historical Example**: Toyota's Lean manufacturing system revolutionized production by emphasizing interconnected feedback loops and continuous improvement. This approach mirrors how we can align personal habits, professional goals, and external influences to create synergy in our lives.

- **Your Application**: If your work drains your energy, it can ripple into your relationships and personal growth. Conversely, a fulfilling personal hobby can re-energize you for professional challenges. View your life as an integrated whole, not isolated silos.

Practical Steps to Build Your Purpose Ecosystem

1. **Clarify Your Core Values:**
   - Use tools like the Personal Values Assessment to identify what truly matters to you.
   - Reflect on historical figures or organizations you admire. What values guided their decisions?

2. **Set Intentional Goals:**
   - Break down long-term aspirations into actionable steps. For example, if your purpose involves sustainability, set goals like reducing your workplace's carbon footprint or launching a community initiative.

3. **Optimize Your Environment:**
   - Declutter your workspace to reduce distractions. Add elements like natural light, plants, or motivational quotes.
   - Digitally, organize your tools and apps to streamline productivity and eliminate digital noise.

4. **Cultivate Supportive Relationships:**
   - Conduct a relationship audit. Identify people who uplift and inspire you, and invest more time with them.
   - Join professional networks or communities aligned with your purpose. For example, if your focus is innovation, engage with groups like TED or design-thinking forums.

5. **Commit to Continuous Learning:**
   - Enroll in courses, attend workshops, or read widely on topics related to your purpose. Lifelong learning fuels adaptability and growth.
   - Seek feedback from mentors or peers to refine your approach.

6. **Reflect and Adapt:**
   - Dedicate time weekly or monthly to evaluate your progress. Use prompts like, "What aligned with my values this week? What didn't?"
   - Be open to recalibrating your goals or strategies based on new insights or changes in circumstances.

Living Your Purpose Ecosystem

Your purpose ecosystem is more than a set of tools or routines; it's a living, breathing framework that evolves with you. From the interconnected layers of influence to the driving forces of motivation and the resilience of a growth mindset, every element works together to create a life of alignment and impact.

The lessons of history show us that purpose-driven ecosystems, whether in the life of innovators like Edison or organizations like Toyota, are not built overnight. They require intentional effort, reflection, and a willingness to adapt. By integrating these principles into your life, you create a system where purpose isn't a fleeting idea but a daily reality.

As you nurture your ecosystem, you'll find that challenges become opportunities, goals transform into milestones, and every decision contributes to a life that reflects your true values. Purpose becomes not just what you pursue, but how you live.

Chapter 12

Overcoming Resistance

Resistance, whether internal or external, often stands between where you are and where you aspire to be. It manifests in many forms: fear of failure, anxiety about uncertainty, or even a quiet reluctance to let go of the familiar. Yet resistance is not inherently negative, it is a natural response, rooted in both psychology and biology, that can serve as a powerful indicator of areas requiring attention and growth.

To overcome resistance, especially in the pursuit of purpose, we must delve into its origins, understand the dynamics at play, and adopt strategies to transform it into a catalyst for meaningful progress. This chapter integrates insights from psychological frameworks, neuroscientific research, and real-world applications to help you tackle resistance with intentionality and resilience.

The Psychological Roots of Resistance

At its core, resistance arises from deeply ingrained psychological mechanisms. It is not simply about unwillingness or stubbornness; rather, it is an evolutionary response designed to protect us from perceived threats.

1. **Fear of the Unknown**: Resistance often stems from fear, fear of failure, rejection, or venturing into uncharted territory. For instance, when Galileo first proposed heliocentrism, he faced immense resistance from the Catholic Church, rooted in fear of disrupting

long-standing beliefs and authority. This fear parallels personal resistance when purpose-driven pursuits challenge entrenched norms or expectations.

2. **Cognitive Dissonance**: When new ideas conflict with established beliefs, cognitive dissonance emerges. This discomfort can cause individuals to resist purpose-driven changes, preferring the comfort of consistency over the effort required to reconcile conflicting values. A modern example lies in organizational resistance to sustainability initiatives, where profit-driven mindsets clash with ethical imperatives.

3. **Loss Aversion**: Resistance is often fueled by the psychological principle of loss aversion, the tendency to prioritize avoiding losses over acquiring equivalent gains. For individuals and organizations alike, the fear of losing comfort, status, or stability can outweigh the potential benefits of change.

The Neuroscience of Resistance

Resistance is not just a psychological phenomenon; it has a biological basis in how the brain perceives and responds to change. Neuroscience provides key insights into why we resist and how we can reframe resistance to encourage growth.

1. **Amygdala Activation**: The amygdala, the brain's threat detector, becomes hyperactive when faced with change, triggering a fight-or-flight response. This explains the visceral discomfort associated with resistance, whether it's resisting a new role or hesitating to pursue a long-held dream.

2. **Prefrontal Cortex Engagement**: The prefrontal cortex, responsible for higher-order thinking, problem-solving,

and planning, must override the amygdala to approach resistance rationally. Engaging this part of the brain through intentional practices like reflection, visualization, or guided planning can transform fear into focused action.

3. **Neuroplasticity and Adaptation**: Resistance can be reprogrammed through **neuroplasticity**, the brain's ability to form new neural connections in response to experiences. By repeatedly confronting resistance and reframing it as an opportunity, individuals can create new mental pathways that support adaptability and resilience.

Transforming Resistance: Strategies and Frameworks

Overcoming resistance requires more than willpower; it demands a structured approach that combines psychological understanding, neuroscience, and actionable strategies. Below are evidence-based methods to address resistance effectively.

1. **Cultivate Curiosity:** Curiosity can dismantle resistance by shifting focus from fear to discovery. When individuals ask questions like "What can I learn from this?" or "How might this challenge help me grow?" they reframe resistance as an opportunity.

    - **Historical Example**: Albert Einstein, often labelled as a poor student early in life, embraced curiosity as a guiding principle. His relentless questioning of established theories led to groundbreaking insights, illustrating how curiosity can override resistance.

    - **Actionable Tip**: Approach resistance with a sense of wonder. Create a list of questions about the potential benefits of the change or challenge you're facing and explore answers through research or discussion.

2. **Engage Stakeholders:** In organizational contexts, resistance often arises when individuals feel excluded from decision-making processes. Involving stakeholders in defining the path forward fosters ownership and reduces pushback.

   - **Historical Example:** When Toyota introduced its Lean manufacturing system, it engaged workers at every level to refine and optimize processes. This participatory approach not only minimized resistance but also led to groundbreaking efficiency gains.

   - **Actionable Tip:** Whether in personal or professional settings, involve others in the process. If resistance arises at work, propose brainstorming sessions or feedback loops to make the process collaborative.

3. **Celebrate Incremental Wins:** Breaking down larger goals into smaller, achievable steps reduces overwhelm and creates momentum. Each small success reinforces positive behaviors and diminishes resistance.

   - **Historical Example:** NASA's Apollo program, which culminated in the moon landing, succeeded by setting incremental goals: first orbiting Earth, then the moon, and finally landing. Each milestone built confidence and reduced resistance to seemingly insurmountable challenges.

- **Actionable Tip**: Identify one small, actionable step toward overcoming resistance. Celebrate its completion, and use the resulting confidence to tackle the next step.

4. **Address Emotional Barriers:** Understanding and addressing emotional resistance is essential. Empathy and emotional regulation can transform fear into trust and openness.

    - **Historical Example**: During the American Civil Rights Movement, leaders like Martin Luther King Jr. addressed societal resistance with empathy and dialogue, focusing on shared humanity to dismantle emotional and cultural barriers.

    - **Actionable Tip**: Practice mindfulness to manage emotional responses. When resistance arises, pause to identify the emotions driving it and respond with compassion rather than judgment.

5. **Reframe Challenges:** Resistance often arises from viewing change as a threat. Reframing challenges as opportunities for growth can shift perspectives.

    - **Historical Example**: Netflix's transition from DVD rentals to streaming faced resistance internally and externally. By reframing this shift as an opportunity to lead the industry, the company transformed potential failure into global success.

    - **Actionable Tip**: Write down the worst-case scenario of pursuing change, followed by the best-case scenario. Reflect on how the potential benefits outweigh the risks.

Practical Steps for Daily Implementation

1. **Daily Reflection**: Spend 5-10 minutes each day journaling about moments of resistance. Ask yourself what triggered it, what you learned from it, and how you can move forward.

2. **Visualization**: Picture yourself successfully navigating the change you're resisting. Neuroscience shows that mental rehearsal strengthens neural pathways, making the transition feel more attainable.

3. **Seek Feedback**: Regularly engage trusted mentors, colleagues, or friends to discuss your resistance. Outside perspectives can illuminate blind spots and offer practical solutions.

4. **Experiment and Iterate**: Treat resistance as a hypothesis to test. Take small steps to challenge it, reflect on the outcomes, and adjust your approach accordingly.

5. **Create Support Systems**: Surround yourself with people who encourage growth and adaptability. Their influence can help you reframe resistance as a shared journey.

Overcoming Resistance: The Path Forward

Resistance is not an obstacle to be bulldozed but a teacher to be engaged. By understanding its psychological roots and neurological mechanisms, we can approach resistance with curiosity, empathy, and intention. From historical examples of societal transformations to personal breakthroughs, resistance has always been a precursor to growth.

In embracing resistance, you transform fear into fuel, hesitation into action, and uncertainty into discovery. The path to purpose is not without its challenges, but it is in facing and reframing these challenges that the most profound growth occurs. Every step taken toward understanding and overcoming resistance is a step closer to living a life aligned with your deepest values and aspirations.

Part 5

Managing Challenges on the Path to Purpose

Managing Challenges to Achieve Goals

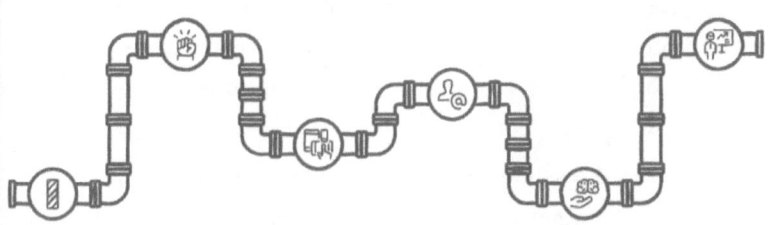

Living a life guided by purpose is a pursuit that resonates deeply with our inherent need to find meaning. The decision to align one's career and existence with purpose is not merely a choice but a profound declaration of intent, an assertion that life is about more than survival or superficial achievement. It is a journey that transforms how we perceive work, relationships, and even ourselves. Yet, this journey, though rewarding, requires deliberate effort, reflection, and resilience.

This section of the book invites you to embark on a deeper exploration of what it means to live purposefully amidst the inevitable complexities of modern life. It is not about prescribing a formula for success but about laying the foundation for a mindset that thrives in the face of uncertainty. To live with purpose is to embrace life's unpredictability with clarity, to navigate choices with intention, and to find joy not just in the destination but in the very act of moving toward something meaningful.

As we delve into the chapters ahead, the focus shifts to practical strategies and transformative perspectives that equip you to navigate this path. From addressing the internal doubts that arise when pursuing purpose to understanding how to sustain alignment in the long run, these chapters are designed to guide you through the intricacies of purposeful living.

The road to purpose is deeply personal, requiring you to peel back the layers of societal expectations, fear, and self-doubt. It demands that you question what success means to you and challenge the narratives you've been taught about work, achievement, and fulfillment. At its core, living with purpose is not about adding more to your life but about stripping away the distractions and falsehoods that obscure what truly matters.

As you turn the page to the next chapter, you will find tools and insights that are as much about reflection as they are about action. This part of the book is an invitation, a call to embrace your path with courage and clarity, knowing that every step you take brings you closer to the life you were meant to live. Let this journey toward managing the challenges of purpose be one of self-discovery, empowerment, and unwavering resolve.

Chapter 13

Beyond the Breaking Point: How Work Challenges Shape Purpose and Performance

Pursuing a purpose-driven career or life is not a serene path illuminated by clarity at every step. Instead, it's a road that often feels riddled with jagged stones, unexpected detours, and steep climbs. The challenges faced along this path are not just external, market fluctuations, job insecurity, or resource scarcity, they are deeply internal too, woven into the very fabric of how humans process uncertainty, fear, and ambition.

Challenges, in their rawest form, are the natural companions of purpose. They arise as the human psyche grapples with the tension between aspiration and reality, between who we are and who we wish to become. To understand the difficulties inherent in building a purpose-driven life, we must look not just at the obstacles themselves, but at the deeper forces within us that shape how we experience and interpret these challenges.

The neuroscience of how humans react to challenges reveals much about why they can feel so overwhelming. When faced with adversity, the brain's amygdala triggers a flood of stress hormones like cortisol and adrenaline, activating a fight-or-flight response. This system, designed to keep our ancestors alive when faced with physical threats, remains active even in today's far more nuanced environments. The same instinct that once helped evade predators now fires up when we confront a critical deadline or experience a professional setback. The physiological reaction, the racing heart, the tightening chest, the inability to focus, makes challenges feel larger than life, as though they hold the power to upend everything we've worked for.

The emotional component of challenges compounds their weight. Purpose-driven individuals, by definition, tie a deep sense of identity and meaning to their work. When faced with obstacles, these challenges don't merely feel like professional hurdles; they feel personal. A setback isn't just a missed target; it can feel like a failure of one's values or ambitions. This emotional depth makes purpose-driven challenges uniquely difficult to navigate, as they strike at the core of who we are and what we hope to achieve.

Research by cognitive scientists, including the work of Dr. Lisa Feldman Barrett, highlights how our brains construct emotions based on past experiences. If you've encountered failure before, especially in situations tied to purpose or identity, your brain uses those memories to predict how current challenges will unfold. This process, while rooted in efficiency, often amplifies fear and anxiety, making present difficulties feel heavier than they might objectively be. The human mind doesn't merely react to challenges; it anticipates their consequences, often inflating their scope and impact.

Challenges are not only psychological but also societal. The modern work environment adds its own complexities to the pursuit of purpose. Toxic work cultures, hierarchical power dynamics, and the relentless emphasis on productivity over well-being create environments where challenges feel like insurmountable barriers. A leader's indifference or a colleague's competitiveness can make even small setbacks feel like monumental failures. Studies on workplace behavior, like those conducted by Dr. Christina Maslach on burnout, show how these environments can erode not just productivity but the very sense of purpose that initially inspired individuals to choose their career paths.

Additionally, societal narratives about success often clash with the realities of a purpose-driven life. Mainstream culture frequently celebrates speed, efficiency, and measurable outcomes, leaving little room for the slower, introspective work of finding meaning and fulfillment. This dissonance between external expectations and internal desires can make the pursuit of purpose feel like swimming against a current that constantly pushes for conformity. Challenges in such contexts feel less like hurdles to be overcome and more like the natural state of things, an ongoing battle to assert values in a world that often undervalues them.

Even within the self, purpose creates friction. The very act of committing to a meaningful path invites an internal dialogue between ambition and doubt. Neuroscientists like Dr. Andrew Huberman have highlighted how uncertainty activates the brain's threat detection systems, creating a physiological reaction to ambiguous outcomes. For purpose-driven individuals, this translates into a near-constant hum of questioning: Am I on the right path? Is this worth it? Will I achieve what I set out to do? These questions, while crucial for reflection, can become paralyzing when layered with external pressures and internal insecurities.

The challenges aren't confined to the individual, either. They ripple outward, affecting relationships, communities, and organizations. Purpose-driven people often find themselves at odds with systems that prioritize profit or efficiency over meaning and impact. Their values may challenge the status quo, creating friction with those around them. This tension can manifest in strained workplace relationships, professional isolation, or even outright rejection of their ideas. The challenge here isn't just to navigate external resistance but to maintain belief in one's purpose when faced with doubt or pushback from others.

On a more existential level, challenges related to purpose tap into the broader human condition. Philosopher Viktor Frankl, in his seminal work *Man's Search for Meaning*, described how purpose provides a buffer against suffering. Yet, this same reliance on purpose can magnify challenges. When purpose becomes the lens through which all actions are evaluated, every misstep or failure feels magnified. It's as though the stakes are perpetually high, with every challenge carrying the weight of existential significance.

There is also the paradoxical nature of challenges tied to purpose. The pursuit of a meaningful life requires deep investment, of time, energy, and emotion, but it is precisely this investment that makes challenges so impactful. The more we care about something, the harder it becomes to face adversity within it. This paradox creates a feedback loop: the more meaningful the goal, the greater the risk of disappointment, yet the very existence of such challenges affirms the significance of the endeavor.

Challenges, then, are both the price and the proof of a purpose-driven life. They demand resilience, yes, but more importantly, they demand that we confront our own expectations, fears, and motivations. They are mirrors reflecting not just the obstacles we face but the values and aspirations that make those obstacles worth confronting. In this way, challenges are not merely disruptions on the path to purpose; they are integral to the journey itself, shaping the way forward even as they test our resolve.

The chapters that follow will delve into the intricacies of managing these challenges, offering frameworks, tools, and insights to help navigate the complexities of a life lived with intention. For now, it is enough to recognize the weight of challenges, not as deterrents but as defining moments in the pursuit of a meaningful existence. In their presence, we find both the depth of our struggles and the measure of our commitment to a life that matters.

Challenges of Living with Purpose: A Closer Look

The pursuit of purpose-driven work is a deeply human aspiration, but it brings with it a unique set of challenges that intertwine with our neural processes and cognitive patterns. Let us delve deeper into these challenges by unravelling their roots in neuroscience, cognitive science, and psychology.

1. **Fear of Failure**
   - **Neural Mechanisms:** The brain's amygdala, a critical part of the limbic system, becomes hyperactive when we face the possibility of failure. This triggers the release of stress hormones like cortisol and adrenaline, heightening our fight-or-flight response. While this response was adaptive for physical survival, it can become counterproductive in modern contexts, leading to avoidance rather than engagement.
   - **Cognitive Bias:** Fear of failure is often magnified by the brain's negativity bias, which causes us to overestimate risks and underestimate our ability to

cope with setbacks. This bias can skew our perception, making challenges seem insurmountable.

- **Psychological Toll:** Chronic activation of the fear response fosters a mindset of self-preservation rather than growth, which can stifle creativity and risk-taking, essential components of purposeful work.

2. **Perfectionism**

    - **Neuroscientific Basis:** Perfectionism involves excessive activation of the prefrontal cortex, where planning and decision-making occur. This overactivation creates rigid neural loops that drive constant self-monitoring and self-criticism.

    - **Cognitive Distortions:** Perfectionists often exhibit all-or-nothing thinking, a cognitive distortion that leads them to view any deviation from their ideal as a complete failure. This creates a mental feedback loop that reinforces anxiety and procrastination.

    - **Emotional Drain:** The pursuit of unattainable standards results in an overtaxed nervous system, contributing to exhaustion, reduced performance, and emotional burnout.

3. **Identity Conflict**

    - **Neural Integration Challenges:** The human brain processes self-identity through interconnected networks involving the prefrontal cortex and the posterior cingulate cortex. When purpose-driven aspirations clash with societal expectations or self-perceptions, these networks struggle to reconcile conflicting inputs, creating cognitive dissonance.

- **Impact on Self-Worth:** Identity conflicts can lead to a fragmented sense of self, where individuals feel torn between external validation and internal alignment. This mental tension often results in decreased motivation and self-esteem.

- **Long-Term Consequences:** Over time, unresolved identity conflicts can rewire neural pathways, embedding patterns of doubt and indecision into daily thought processes.

4. **External Resistance**

   - **Neuroscientific Basis of Social Pain:** External resistance, whether from unsupportive colleagues, leaders, or systems, activates the brain's anterior cingulate cortex, the same region involved in processing physical pain. This overlap explains why social rejection or opposition can feel viscerally painful.

   - **Group Dynamics and Conformity:** Human brains are wired to prioritize group belonging, as evidenced by activation of the ventral striatum during social acceptance. Resistance from others disrupts this neural reward system, creating feelings of isolation and self-doubt.

   - **Behavioral Consequences:** Prolonged exposure to external resistance often leads to withdrawal, diminished trust, or overcompensation through excessive effort to gain approval, all of which detract from purpose-driven progress.

5. **Emotional Exhaustion and Burnout**
    - **Physiological Mechanisms:** Chronic stress from purpose-driven overcommitment keeps the hypothalamic-pituitary-adrenal (HPA) axis in a state of hyperactivation. This leads to elevated cortisol levels, which impair memory, concentration, and decision-making over time.
    - **Neural Fatigue:** Burnout reduces activity in the brain's prefrontal cortex, compromising executive functions such as planning, prioritization, and emotional regulation. Simultaneously, it increases amygdala activity, amplifying stress responses.
    - **Cognitive Impacts:** Emotional exhaustion fosters a state of learned helplessness, where individuals perceive challenges as insurmountable and begin to disengage from their goals.

6. **Fear of the Unknown**
    - **Brain's Aversion to Uncertainty:** The human brain perceives uncertainty as a threat, activating the amygdala and releasing stress hormones. This creates a physiological state of hypervigilance, where even small uncertainties feel overwhelming.
    - **Cognitive Paralysis:** Uncertainty inhibits the brain's decision-making pathways, particularly in the prefrontal cortex. This results in analysis paralysis, where individuals get stuck evaluating options without taking action.
    - **Emotional Resistance:** Fear of the unknown often triggers avoidance behaviors, reinforcing neural

pathways associated with safety-seeking rather than risk-taking and growth.

7. **Resource Scarcity**
    - **Cognitive Load Theory:** Scarcity, whether of time, money, or mentorship, overloads the brain's working memory, making it harder to focus on long-term goals. This cognitive strain reduces efficiency and increases susceptibility to errors.

    - **Stress Amplification:** Scarcity keeps the brain's HPA axis on high alert, creating a chronic stress response that undermines creativity and problem-solving.

    - **Perception of Lack:** Neuroscientific studies show that resource scarcity triggers the insular cortex, which processes feelings of deprivation. This neural activation can make challenges feel more daunting than they are.

8. **Cultural and Societal Expectations**
    - **Social Conditioning and Neural Pathways:** Societal norms are deeply ingrained through repeated exposure, creating robust neural circuits that reinforce conformity. Deviating from these norms often triggers feelings of guilt or shame, rooted in the brain's default mode network (DMN).

    - **Impact on Risk-Taking:** Cultural pressure to adhere to traditional metrics of success inhibits the brain's exploratory pathways, reducing the likelihood of pursuing unconventional, purpose-driven goals.

- **Emotional Cost:** The clash between societal expectations and personal aspirations can activate the brain's limbic system, heightening emotional distress and fostering self-doubt.

9. **Lack of Immediate Gratification**

    - **Delayed Reward Systems:** Purpose-driven endeavours often involve long-term goals that lack immediate payoffs. This delays activation of the brain's reward circuits, reducing the motivational effects of dopamine.

    - **Emotional Drain:** The absence of frequent positive reinforcement can lead to frustration and a sense of futility, particularly in environments that emphasize quick wins.

    - **Cognitive Adaptation:** Sustaining effort without immediate rewards requires significant prefrontal cortex engagement, which can deplete mental resources over time.

10. **Inner Saboteurs**

    - **Neural Self-Criticism:** Negative self-talk activates the brain's default mode network in ways that amplify feelings of inadequacy. Over time, this rewires neural pathways, reinforcing patterns of self-doubt.

    - **Impostor Syndrome:** The persistent belief of being unworthy activates the brain's anterior cingulate cortex, fostering a sense of vigilance and fear of exposure.

- **Behavioral Consequences:** Inner saboteurs often manifest as avoidance, procrastination, or overcompensation, all of which detract from purposeful progress.

11. Misaligned Environments

- **Brain's Response to Mismatch:** When values clash with workplace cultures or systems, the brain's stress response system becomes chronically activated. This reduces cognitive flexibility and problem-solving abilities.

- **Social Isolation:** Misaligned environments often diminish oxytocin levels, weakening feelings of trust and connection.

- **Impact on Motivation:** Over time, these environments erode intrinsic motivation, making it harder to sustain purposeful efforts.

12. Overcommitment

- **Cognitive Fragmentation:** Juggling multiple tasks divides attention and overtaxes the brain's working memory, reducing overall efficiency and clarity.

- **Physiological Strain:** Chronic overcommitment keeps the body in a heightened state of arousal, depleting energy reserves and impairing decision-making.

- **Emotional Cost:** Overcommitment often leads to feelings of guilt and inadequacy, as individuals struggle to meet their own expectations.

13. Existential Doubt

- **Neural Processing of Big Questions:** Existential doubt activates the brain's DMN, drawing attention inward to self-reflective and philosophical thoughts. While this can foster insight, excessive introspection can create rumination loops.

- **Emotional Weight:** Doubts about purpose amplify the brain's limbic responses, heightening feelings of anxiety and uncertainty.

- **Paralysis by Analysis:** The constant questioning of meaning and direction reduces the brain's ability to take decisive action, leaving individuals stuck in cycles of inaction.

Each of these challenges is deeply rooted in the complex interplay of neuroscience, cognitive processes, and societal influences. By understanding the brain's mechanisms and the psychological frameworks that underpin these obstacles, we gain a richer perspective on the difficulties of living a purpose-driven life.

Chapter 14

Breaking Through Barriers: A Step-by-Step Guide to Managing Purposeful Challenges

The journey of navigating challenges on the path to purpose is akin to traversing an intricate labyrinth, one where the twists and turns are shaped by deeply ingrained beliefs, societal expectations, and the enigmatic workings of the human mind. Understanding what it means to navigate these challenges goes beyond merely overcoming obstacles. It involves a transformative process of self-awareness, emotional resilience, and deliberate action, informed by the cutting-edge insights of neuroscience and psychology.

What Does Managing Challenges Mean?

At its core, managing challenges means consciously addressing the barriers that inhibit one's alignment with a purposeful life. These barriers may manifest as fear of failure, emotional burnout, identity conflicts, or resistance from societal norms. The act of navigating requires the interplay of introspection, adaptability, and a willingness to confront discomfort. It is not just about surviving challenges but about using them as catalysts for growth and self-discovery.

In navigating these challenges, individuals must first understand that obstacles are not static. They are fluid, influenced by both internal narratives and external environments. Neuroscience provides an invaluable lens through which we can view this process, shedding light on how the brain perceives, processes, and reacts to challenges, and, crucially, how it can be rewired to overcome them.

The Neuroscientific Lens on Challenges

Modern neuroscience has revolutionized our understanding of how humans face and respond to adversity. Challenges on the path to purpose are often processed in the brain as threats, activating primitive survival mechanisms that prioritize immediate safety over long-term aspirations. However, the brain is also remarkably plastic, capable of reshaping its neural networks to facilitate growth, resilience, and purposeful action.

1. The Role of the Amygdala: The Seat of Fear

The amygdala, a small almond-shaped structure deep within the brain, is often referred to as the brain's "alarm system." It plays a pivotal role in processing fear and anxiety, particularly when faced with uncertainty or perceived threats. Challenges such as fear of failure or social judgment activate the amygdala, triggering the body's fight-or-flight response.

While this response is essential for survival, it can become a hindrance when overactivated. Chronic stress from prolonged challenges can lead to hyperactivity in the amygdala, resulting in heightened anxiety, avoidance behaviors, and emotional exhaustion. Neuroscientists like Dr. Joseph LeDoux have highlighted that managing the amygdala's response is key to navigating challenges effectively. Techniques such as mindfulness and cognitive reframing have been shown to reduce amygdala activity, fostering a calmer, more measured approach to adversity.

2. The Prefrontal Cortex: The Executive Decision-Maker

The prefrontal cortex, located at the front of the brain, is the command center for higher-order cognitive functions such as decision-making, planning, and emotional regulation. Unlike the amygdala, which reacts impulsively, the prefrontal cortex evaluates challenges rationally, weighing long-term goals against short-term fears.

Neuroscientist Dr. Richard Davidson's research emphasizes the role of the prefrontal cortex in fostering resilience. Strengthening this area through deliberate practices like meditation, problem-solving exercises, and goal-setting enables individuals to navigate challenges with clarity and focus. The prefrontal cortex empowers individuals to override fear-based impulses from the amygdala, steering them toward purposeful action.

3. Neuroplasticity: The Brain's Capacity for Change

One of the most profound discoveries in neuroscience is the concept of neuroplasticity, the brain's ability to form and reorganize synaptic connections in response to experience. This adaptability underscores the transformative potential of challenges. By confronting and working through adversity, individuals can literally reshape their neural pathways, reinforcing patterns of resilience, creativity, and determination.

Dr. Norman Doidge's work on neuroplasticity highlights that repeated engagement with challenges, paired with positive reinforcement, strengthens neural circuits associated with problem-solving and emotional regulation. This means that each challenge overcome not only builds mental fortitude but also primes the brain for future success.

4. The Default Mode Network: Self-Reflection and Meaning-Making

The Default Mode Network (DMN) is a network of brain regions active during introspection, self-referential thinking, and envisioning the future. When individuals reflect on their purpose and how challenges align with their goals, the DMN facilitates deeper understanding and integration of experiences.

Dr. Marcus Raichle, a leading researcher on the DMN, has shown that engaging this network through reflective practices like journaling or meditation enhances self-awareness and clarity. This introspection allows individuals to contextualize challenges, viewing them not as barriers but as stepping stones to greater meaning.

Psychological Perspectives on Challenges

In addition to neuroscience, psychological theories provide valuable insights into navigating purpose-driven challenges. These perspectives illuminate the interplay between cognition, emotion, and behavior, offering strategies to reinterpret and respond to adversity.

1. Cognitive Dissonance and Adaptation

Cognitive dissonance arises when there is a conflict between one's beliefs and actions. For example, an individual striving for a purpose-driven career may experience discomfort when working in a role misaligned with their values. This dissonance often triggers resistance, procrastination, or self-doubt.

Psychologist Leon Festinger's theory of cognitive dissonance suggests that resolving this discomfort requires either altering one's beliefs or changing one's actions. Purposeful navigation involves aligning actions with deeply held values, reducing dissonance and fostering a sense of integrity.

2. Emotional Resilience and Hope

Dr. Barbara Fredrickson's research on positive psychology highlights the role of hope and optimism in overcoming challenges. Hope acts as a psychological buffer, enabling individuals to envision a better future even in the face of adversity. This forward-looking mindset not only reduces stress but also motivates proactive problem-solving.

3. The Growth Mindset

Carol Dweck's concept of the growth mindset, believing that abilities and intelligence can be developed, offers a powerful framework for navigating challenges. Viewing obstacles as opportunities for growth encourages persistence, adaptability, and a willingness to learn from failure.

The Interplay of Neuroscience and Psychology

The convergence of neuroscience and psychology reveals that navigating challenges is both a mental and physiological process. The brain's plasticity ensures that individuals are never static in their abilities, while psychological resilience enables them to reinterpret adversity in constructive ways. Together, these insights highlight the immense potential within each person to transform challenges into milestones on the path to purpose.

As we continue exploring practical strategies in the next sections, it becomes clear that navigating purposeful challenges is not about avoiding discomfort. It is about embracing it as a natural part of growth, harnessing the brain's capabilities, and fostering a mindset that sees every obstacle as an opportunity for evolution.

A Scientific Step-by-Step Action Guide to Overcome Challenges on the Path to Purpose (Elaborated Action Plan)

Overcoming challenges on the path to purpose requires deep introspection, intentional action, and a clear understanding of the brain's mechanisms. Below is an expanded guide detailing scientifically proven strategies and their application. Each step provides an in-depth action plan to help integrate these strategies into daily life.

Step 1: Strengthen Self-Awareness Through Advanced Techniques

Science Behind It: Self-awareness is driven by the **default mode network (DMN)**, active during reflection and introspection, and the **anterior cingulate cortex (ACC)**, which helps regulate emotions and detect errors. Strengthened self-awareness lays the foundation for understanding personal motivations and aligning actions with purpose.

Action Plan:

1. **Deep Self-Exploration Exercises:**
    - Use tools like the **VIA Survey of Character Strengths** or **Clifton Strengths** to identify core strengths and values. Take time to analyze these results and write down patterns that emerge, such as recurring themes of service, creativity, or innovation.
    - Pair these insights with open-ended reflective questions like:
        - "What am I naturally good at, and how does it make me feel?"
        - "When have I felt the most fulfilled, and what was I doing?"

- Dedicate 30 minutes weekly to revisit and refine your understanding of your strengths and values.

2. **Narrative Therapy Journaling:**
    - Write your life story in stages: childhood, adolescence, and adulthood. For each stage, list key experiences, what they taught you, and how they shaped your values.
    - Identify moments when your actions aligned with your purpose and moments when they didn't. Explore the emotional and cognitive impact of these experiences.
    - Keep a dedicated journal to track evolving insights about your purpose and revisit entries to notice patterns over time.

Step 2: Create a Resilience Toolkit

Science Behind It: Resilience is modulated by the **ventrolateral prefrontal cortex (vmPFC)**, which regulates emotional responses by suppressing overactivity in the amygdala. A well-developed resilience toolkit helps manage stress and fosters adaptability.

Action Plan:

1. **Gratitude Anchoring:**
    - Begin each morning by writing three specific things you are grateful for and explicitly link them to current challenges. For instance:
        - "I am grateful for the opportunity to grow through this project, even though it's demanding."

- Keep a gratitude journal and review it weekly to reinforce positive thinking patterns.
    - Research suggests gratitude practices enhance serotonin and dopamine production, building emotional resilience.

2. **Emotional Buffering Rituals:**
    - Develop a personalized pre-stress routine, such as listening to calming instrumental music, practicing yoga, or visualizing a peaceful setting. These practices calm the nervous system before high-stress situations.
    - Schedule regular breaks throughout your workday. Use techniques like **Pomodoro (25 minutes of work followed by a 5-minute break)** to prevent burnout and improve focus.

Step 3: Leverage Mental Contrasting

Science Behind It: Mental contrasting leverages the brain's **prefrontal cortex** and **hippocampus** to bridge the gap between current reality and desired outcomes. It strengthens goal-directed behavior by reinforcing neural pathways associated with planning and problem-solving.

Action Plan:

3. **WOOP Method (Wish, Outcome, Obstacle, Plan):**
    - Write down your ultimate wish (e.g., "To transition into a career aligned with my purpose").
    - Visualize the best possible outcome in detail: "I see myself thriving in a role where I impact others positively."

- Identify key obstacles, both external and internal: "Fear of failure" or "Lack of resources."

- Create actionable plans for each obstacle:

  o If internal: "I will practice self-compassion and seek mentorship to address my fears."

  o If external: "I will set aside 10% of my income monthly to fund courses."

- Repeat the WOOP exercise weekly to refine goals and assess progress.

4. **Scenario Mapping:**

   - Use decision trees to map potential outcomes of key challenges. For instance:

     o Outcome A: "Successfully pitch a new project."

     o Outcome B: "Receive constructive criticism and refine the idea."

   - Analyze the risks and rewards of each scenario and list immediate next steps.

Step 4: Enhance Cognitive Flexibility

Science Behind It: Cognitive flexibility, governed by the **dorsolateral prefrontal cortex (dlPFC)**, enables individuals to shift perspectives and adapt to new challenges. It fosters creativity and mitigates rigid thinking.

Action Plan:

5. **Perspective-Taking Exercises:**

   - Practice reframing a current challenge from multiple viewpoints. For instance:

- From your perspective: "This setback challenges me to learn and grow."
- From a mentor's perspective: "This is a normal part of developing expertise."
- From an outsider's perspective: "This challenge is a temporary hurdle."
- Engage in role-playing scenarios with a trusted friend to refine your ability to view situations from different angles.

6. **Unconventional Problem-Solving:**
   - Dedicate one brainstorming session per week to generate at least five "wild" or unconventional solutions to a problem.
   - Use mind-mapping tools to connect these solutions with feasible steps.

Step 5: Cultivate Social and Emotional Support

Science Behind It: Social interactions stimulate **oxytocin** production, reducing stress and promoting trust. Building a supportive network reinforces emotional resilience and provides practical help.

Action Plan:

1. **Develop an Accountability Group:**
   - Form a small group of peers who share similar goals. Meet bi-weekly to discuss challenges, exchange resources, and celebrate progress.
   - Assign accountability partners within the group to check in weekly via calls or messages.

2. **Active Listening Practice:**
   - During conversations, focus entirely on the speaker, asking clarifying questions and reflecting their emotions back to them.
   - Commit to at least one "active listening session" weekly where you practice these skills deliberately.

Step 6: Master Stress Regulation

Science Behind It: Chronic stress triggers overactivation of the amygdala and suppresses the prefrontal cortex. Stress management techniques reset the nervous system, enabling clearer thinking.

Action Plan:

1. **Breathwork Techniques:**
   - Practice **4-7-8 breathing**: Inhale for 4 seconds, hold for 7 seconds, exhale for 8 seconds. Do this for 5 minutes daily.
   - Integrate breathing exercises into stressful moments, like before meetings or difficult conversations.

2. **Nature-Based Stress Relief:**
   - Spend at least 30 minutes outdoors daily. Combine this with reflective walks to process challenges.
   - Choose environments with water or greenery, as they have been shown to reduce cortisol levels more effectively.

Step 7: Build Momentum with Incremental Success

Science Behind It: Incremental successes activate dopaminergic pathways, creating a positive feedback loop of motivation and engagement.

Action Plan:

1. **Daily Task Lists:**
   - Break large goals into bite-sized tasks. For example:
     - Instead of "Finish the project proposal," list: "Draft outline," "Research three references," "Write introduction."
   - Prioritize three high-impact tasks daily and celebrate their completion.

2. **Track Progress Visually:**
   - Use apps or physical trackers to monitor progress. Highlight milestones achieved to reinforce a sense of accomplishment.

Step 8: Reframe Failure as Learning

Science Behind It: The **anterior cingulate cortex (ACC)** signals the brain to adjust behavior in response to failure. Reframing failure promotes adaptability and strengthens resilience.

Action Plan:

1. **Post-Failure Reflection:**
   - After setbacks, write a "failure analysis" journal entry:
     - What happened?

- o What did I learn?
- o How will I adapt moving forward?
- End with a self-compassion statement like: "Failure is part of growth."

2. **Create a "Growth Timeline":**
   - Document failures alongside subsequent successes to visualize how setbacks contribute to long-term achievements.

Step 9: Establish a Ritual for Reconnecting with Purpose

Science Behind It: Purpose reactivation engages the **ventral striatum**, reinforcing motivation and long-term goal alignment.

Action Plan:

1. **Morning Intentions:**
   - Dedicate 5 minutes each morning to state your purpose and how the day's actions align with it. For instance:
     - o "Today, I will focus on improving collaboration, as it aligns with my goal of building impactful relationships."
   - Use affirmations to reinforce commitment, like: "I am capable of creating meaningful change."

2. **Weekly Purpose Audit:**
   - Set aside 30 minutes at the end of the week to review your actions. Ask:
     - o "Did my tasks align with my purpose?"
     - o "What adjustments can I make for next week?"

Step 10: Develop a Personal Narrative

Science Behind It: Creating and refining your personal narrative engages the **hippocampus**, responsible for memory and integration, and the **medial prefrontal cortex (mPFC)**, which connects self-referential thinking with goal-directed actions. This process provides clarity, reinforces motivation, and establishes a coherent identity.

Action Plan (Expanded):

1. **Craft Your Story of Growth:**
    - Write a narrative that highlights key moments of growth, resilience, and purpose in your life. For example:
        - "I faced significant challenges during my early career, but they taught me adaptability and perseverance."
        - Frame obstacles as stepping stones to where you are now and align them with your current goals.

2. **Refine and Share Your Story:**
    - Practice sharing your story with a mentor, peer, or group. This reinforces your purpose and helps you internalize your journey.
    - Update your narrative quarterly to reflect new experiences, ensuring it evolves with you.

Step 11: Prioritize Energy Management Over Time Management

Science Behind It: Energy levels are influenced by the brain's **circadian rhythm**, which regulates sleep, alertness, and productivity. Managing energy, rather than just time, ensures peak performance and reduces burnout.

Action Plan (Expanded):

1. **Track Energy Patterns:**
   - For one week, record your energy levels at three intervals (morning, afternoon, evening). Identify patterns, such as when you feel most focused or sluggish.
   - Align demanding tasks with high-energy periods and reserve lower-energy times for routine or creative tasks.

2. **Adopt Strategic Recovery Practices:**
   - Take short breaks every 90 minutes to reset your focus, as recommended by ultradian rhythm research.
   - Incorporate restorative activities like stretching, hydration, or a brief walk outdoors to recharge.

3. **Optimize Sleep Hygiene:**
   - Establish a consistent sleep routine by going to bed and waking up at the same time daily.
   - Limit screen time an hour before sleep to reduce blue light exposure, which disrupts melatonin production.

Step 12: Leverage the Power of Visualization

Science Behind It: Visualization activates the **motor cortex** and **parietal lobes**, which simulate the neural processes involved in executing tasks. This primes the brain for success by reinforcing the pathways needed for achieving goals.

Action Plan (Expanded):

1. **Daily Visualization Practice:**
   - Spend 5 minutes each morning visualizing yourself successfully navigating challenges. Include sensory details:
     - "I see myself confidently presenting the proposal. I hear my voice, calm and steady, and feel a sense of accomplishment."
   - Pair visualization with affirmations to reinforce your mindset.

2. **Pre-Event Visualization:**
   - Before significant tasks (e.g., meetings, presentations), visualize the process step-by-step. Imagine potential obstacles and see yourself overcoming them gracefully.

3. **Long-Term Visualization:**
   - Dedicate time weekly to envision your ultimate goals. For example:
     - "I see myself in a leadership role, inspiring a team aligned with shared values."
   - Reflect on how current efforts contribute to this vision and adjust actions as needed.

Step 13: Cultivate Purpose-Driven Micro Habits

Science Behind It: Micro habits, small intentional actions, leverage **neuroplasticity**, helping the brain rewire itself for lasting change. Consistent micro habits create momentum and reinforce larger behavioral shifts.

Action Plan (Expanded):

1. **Identify Key Micro Habits:**
   - Choose habits directly aligned with your goals, such as:
     - Writing one gratitude note daily.
     - Spending 10 minutes reading industry updates each morning.
   - Ensure these habits are simple and sustainable.

2. **Use Habit Stacking:**
   - Pair new habits with existing routines to increase adherence. For example:
     - After brushing your teeth, spend 2 minutes visualizing your day's purpose.
     - During your afternoon coffee break, review your weekly goals.

3. **Celebrate Consistency:**
   - Track daily habit completion using an app or a journal. Celebrate streaks to reinforce motivation and reward your brain's effort.

Step 14: Build Resilient Neural Pathways Through Intentional Practice

Science Behind It: The brain strengthens connections through repeated practice, a process known as **Hebbian learning**: "neurons that fire together, wire together." Intentional practice refines these pathways, fostering resilience and adaptability.

Action Plan (Expanded):

1. **Focus on One Skill at a Time:**
   - Identify a skill that addresses a current challenge, such as public speaking or conflict resolution.
   - Dedicate 15-30 minutes daily to deliberate practice. Break the skill into sub-components (e.g., tone modulation, posture, active listening) and focus on one at a time.

2. **Seek Real-Time Feedback:**
   - Practice in real-life scenarios and solicit immediate feedback from a mentor or colleague. For example:
     - "Did my presentation connect well with the audience? What could improve?"

3. **Document Progress:**
   - Keep a log of skill development, noting improvements, obstacles, and lessons learned. Review it monthly to track long-term growth.

Step 15: Engage in Acts of Purposeful Service

Science Behind It: Engaging in altruistic activities activates the **ventral striatum** and increases oxytocin levels, enhancing happiness and reinforcing feelings of purpose.

Action Plan (Expanded):

1. **Integrate Service into Daily Life:**
    - Identify small ways to contribute meaningfully, such as mentoring a junior colleague or volunteering at a local organization.
    - Schedule at least one act of service weekly, ensuring it aligns with your values.

2. **Reflect on Impact:**
    - After each act of service, journal about its impact on others and your sense of purpose. For instance:
        - "Helping a coworker with their report reminded me of my commitment to fostering collaboration."

3. **Create a Legacy Mindset:**
    - Envision how your actions today contribute to a lasting impact. Frame decisions around questions like:
        - "How will this choice create a ripple effect for others?"

Expanding Beyond the Steps

These scientifically grounded strategies are not just isolated tools but part of a larger, integrated system. As each step builds on the previous one, the individual creates a momentum of personal growth and resilience that cascades into every area of life. This is not merely about overcoming immediate challenges but transforming how one approaches purpose-driven living entirely. This framework demonstrates that the path to purpose, while fraught with obstacles, is navigable with intentionality, science, and a commitment to self-growth.

Part 6

Lifelong Purpose Evolution

Journey of Purpose Evolution

Youthful Discovery

Adapting Through Challenges

Embracing Transitions

Reflective Growth

Social Impact

Legacy Creation

Purpose is not a fixed destination; it is a living, breathing force that grows and evolves with us. As we journey through life's seasons, facing triumphs, challenges, and transitions, our sense of purpose shifts, reshaping itself to meet the moment. This evolution is not a sign of instability but of adaptability, reflecting the dynamic nature of human existence. Embracing this evolution allows us to remain anchored in meaning, no matter how the tides of life change.

At its core, the lifelong evolution of purpose is a testament to the resilience and ingenuity of the human spirit. Just as we adapt to new environments and forge new connections, we reimagine our purpose, building upon the foundation of who we are and who we aspire to become. Science affirms that our brains are wired for growth and reinvention, constantly reshaping neural pathways in response to new experiences. This capacity for lifelong adaptation empowers us to find purpose in every stage of life, from the ambitions of youth to the reflections of later years.

Purpose evolution is not merely an individual journey; it influences families, communities, and societies. It pushes boundaries, ignites passions, and inspires collective action. From the teenager discovering their first cause to the retiree dedicating their time to mentoring others, the evolution of purpose weaves a powerful narrative of personal growth and social impact.

But this journey is not always linear or simple. There are times when our purpose feels obscured by uncertainty, or when shifting priorities force us to recalibrate. Yet, even in these moments, purpose quietly adapts, waiting to emerge in ways that align with our changing reality. By learning to recognize and embrace these shifts, we unlock a deeper connection to ourselves and the world.

The evolution of purpose is an invitation, to continuously explore, redefine, and act. It is a call to nurture the passions that fuel us and to confront the challenges that shape us. It reminds us that every phase of life holds the potential for growth and meaning, and that our purpose is as expansive as our willingness to pursue it.

As we delve into the lifelong evolution of purpose, let us remember: our purpose is not confined to a single role or goal. It is the thread that connects all chapters of our story, evolving with us, and driving us toward a life of fulfillment and impact. This is not just a journey; it is a legacy, a dynamic force that endures, expands, and leaves an indelible mark on the world.

Chapter 18

Reimagining Purpose at Midlife

A Fork in the Road

Imagine standing at a fork in the road. Behind you lies the journey you've traveled, filled with achievements, challenges, and lessons learned. Ahead lies a path shrouded in mystery, beckoning you to explore new possibilities. This is midlife, a pivotal moment, not of crisis but of opportunity.

For years, society has painted midlife as a time of decline, marked by existential dread and fleeting attempts to reclaim youth. But what if, instead, midlife is a season of awakening? A time to take stock of the life you've lived, honor your experiences, and chart a new course aligned with who you've become. This period, sometimes called "middlescence," mirrors adolescence in its intensity, inviting deep introspection, growth, and transformation.

With insights from neuroscience, psychology, and human experience, this chapter explores how midlife can become a launchpad for reimagining purpose. Through stories, science, and strategies, we'll unravel how this phase of life offers not just challenges but profound opportunities for renewal.

Understanding Midlife Transitions: The Season of Change

Midlife, often encompassing the ages of 40 to 60, is a period marked by change. While some may perceive these transitions as unsettling, they offer an opportunity for growth and renewal.

The shifts that define midlife touch every corner of life, family, physical health, and professional identity, all of which prompt a re-examination of one's sense of self and priorities.

Family Dynamics

Family life often undergoes significant transformation during midlife. Children grow into independence, leaving home to pursue their own paths, a transition known as the "empty nest" phase. While this can bring a sense of loss, it also opens space for parents to rediscover themselves and redefine their relationship as partners beyond their role as caregivers. Conversely, aging parents may require more attention, adding new responsibilities and reshaping familial roles.

These dynamics can inspire individuals to reflect on their core values and relationships. For some, the shift brings a newfound appreciation for personal connections and intergenerational bonds.

Physical Changes

The physical changes of midlife can feel like a confrontation with mortality. Slower metabolisms, emerging health concerns, and changes in appearance often bring a heightened awareness of the body's limitations. However, these shifts can also be a catalyst for positive change. Many people in midlife begin prioritizing wellness, embracing exercise, nutrition, and mindfulness as tools to support longevity and vitality.

Rather than resisting these physical transformations, midlife offers a chance to align lifestyle choices with long-term health goals, cultivating habits that nurture both body and mind.

Career Shifts

Professional identity often evolves in midlife. By this stage, many individuals find themselves less enamored with external markers of success, such as promotions or titles, and more interested in meaningful work that reflects their values. Whether it's pivoting to a new field, scaling back to achieve better work-life balance, or mentoring younger colleagues, midlife professionals increasingly seek roles that offer purpose and fulfillment.

This career evolution can feel daunting, but it's also liberating. It invites midlifers to question: "What truly energizes me? What legacy do I want to leave through my work?"

Re-examining Identity

The interplay of these shifts often leads to what gerontologist Barbara Waxman calls a "midlife reckoning." It's a moment when individuals ask themselves deep, existential questions: "Who am I now? What do I want next?" Far from being a crisis, this reckoning can serve as a powerful invitation to live more intentionally, aligning actions and commitments with an authentic sense of self.

The Science of Transition: Biological Foundations of Midlife Transformation

Midlife transitions are not solely emotional or circumstantial, they are deeply rooted in biological and neurological changes. Understanding these shifts can help demystify the experience and offer strategies to navigate it with greater confidence and grace.

Prefrontal Cortex: Refining Long-Term Thinking

The prefrontal cortex, the brain region responsible for planning, decision-making, and self-regulation, reaches its peak maturity during midlife. This neurological shift enhances our ability to think long-term and weigh the broader consequences of our choices.

This heightened capacity for reflection allows midlifers to pause and consider their priorities, asking themselves whether their current trajectory aligns with their values. It's why so many individuals in this stage seek to make deliberate changes, shifting away from superficial goals toward those with lasting meaning.

Emotional Regulation: Finding Calm Amid Change

As we age, the amygdala, the brain's emotional alarm center, becomes less reactive. This change enables midlifers to navigate challenges with greater emotional stability and perspective. Research suggests that older adults are better equipped to manage stress and resolve conflicts because they are less likely to be overwhelmed by immediate emotional reactions.

This improved emotional regulation helps midlifers embrace transitions, whether in family, health, or career, as opportunities for growth rather than as threats to their identity.

Dopamine Levels: A Shift from Extrinsic to Intrinsic Rewards

Dopamine, a neurotransmitter associated with pleasure and reward, naturally declines with age. This reduction explains why midlifers often feel less motivated by external achievements like promotions or material possessions. Instead, they are drawn to intrinsic rewards such as meaningful relationships, personal growth, and contributions to their community.

This shift in motivation can feel disorienting but is ultimately freeing. It allows individuals to move away from societal pressures and focus on what genuinely brings joy and fulfillment.

The Role of Purpose in Well-Being: Anchoring the Soul

Purpose serves as an essential anchor in the ever-changing currents of life. It provides coherence and direction, especially during the transformative period of midlife, acting as a stabilizing force when familiar structures begin to shift. More than a guiding philosophy, purpose is a profound influence on mental, physical, and neurological well-being, as science increasingly reveals.

Mental Resilience: A Psychological Shield

The presence of purpose in life is a powerful buffer against psychological distress. It provides a sense of meaning and continuity that helps individuals navigate life's inevitable challenges.

Scientific Insights

Martin Pinquart's research on purpose and mental health highlights that individuals with clear life goals experience significantly lower rates of anxiety and depression. Purpose acts as a psychological shield, offering emotional stability during times of transition, such as midlife, when uncertainty can feel overwhelming.

When individuals focus on purpose, they engage the brain's prefrontal cortex, which governs rational thinking and long-term planning. This neurological activation helps reduce overactivity in the amygdala, the region of the brain responsible for fear and anxiety responses. The result is a calmer, more centered approach to life's hurdles.

Practical Implications

Purpose fosters resilience by anchoring individuals in what truly matters. For example, a person navigating the empty nest syndrome might find renewed focus in volunteering for an organization that aligns with their values, turning what could feel like a loss into a source of fulfillment.

Physical Health Benefits: Purpose as a Health Booster

Purpose doesn't just enhance emotional well-being, it profoundly impacts physical health. Numerous studies reveal a strong correlation between living purposefully and improved physiological outcomes.

Reduced Inflammation

Chronic stress is a major contributor to inflammation, which is linked to conditions such as heart disease, arthritis, and diabetes. Purpose helps modulate stress hormones like cortisol, preventing prolonged activation of the body's stress response. A 2016 study in *Psychological Science* found that individuals with high purpose levels exhibited lower inflammatory markers, regardless of age.

Improved Heart Health

Purpose-driven individuals are less likely to develop cardiovascular diseases. A study in *JAMA Cardiology* discovered that people with a strong sense of purpose had a 27% lower risk of dying from heart disease. This link is likely due to the healthier coping mechanisms purpose offers, such as better stress management and lifestyle choices like exercise and diet.

Enhanced Sleep Quality

Purpose has also been linked to improved sleep patterns. A study published in *Sleep Science and Practice* found that older adults with a strong sense of purpose were more likely to experience restful and consistent sleep, which is essential for physical regeneration and mental clarity.

Neural Pathways of Meaning: The Brain on Purpose

Engaging with purpose activates specific neural circuits that not only enhance mental health but also boost cognitive function. Purpose-driven behavior taps into the brain's reward system, providing both emotional satisfaction and neurological benefits.

Activation of the Ventral Striatum

The ventral striatum, a critical component of the brain's reward circuitry, lights up when individuals pursue meaningful goals. This activation releases dopamine, the "feel-good" neurotransmitter, reinforcing purposeful actions and creating a feedback loop that motivates further engagement.

Prefrontal Cortex and Hippocampus Connectivity

Purposeful living also strengthens the connectivity between the prefrontal cortex and the hippocampus. The prefrontal cortex governs decision-making and planning, while the hippocampus is responsible for memory and learning. This enhanced connectivity supports better problem-solving skills, improved memory, and greater cognitive agility, qualities especially valuable during midlife as the brain naturally begins to age.

Neuroplasticity

Engaging in purposeful activities promotes neuroplasticity, the brain's ability to reorganize and form new connections. For example, learning a new skill or pursuing a meaningful hobby at midlife not only enriches one's sense of purpose but also keeps the brain adaptable and resilient.

Strategies for Reimagining Purpose: The Roadmap to Renewal

Reimagining purpose in midlife requires more than wishful thinking, it demands deliberate action. The following strategies blend science, introspection, and real-life examples to guide you through this transformative journey.

1. Self-Reflection: Unearthing What Matters

Self-reflection is the starting point for reimagining purpose. It's about peeling back the layers of societal expectations to discover your authentic self.

- **The Science**: Neuroscientific studies show that the brain's default mode network (DMN), active during self-reflection, helps us connect past experiences with future goals. This process fosters self-awareness and clarity.

- **How to Practice**:

    o **Journaling**: Use prompts like, "What brings me joy?" or "What legacy do I want to leave?" to explore your inner landscape.

    o **Mindfulness**: Meditation enhances introspection, creating mental space to process life's questions.

Real-Life Example: Maria, a 48-year-old teacher, began journaling after her children left for college. Reflecting on her love for storytelling, she launched a community podcast, giving voice to local stories and reigniting her passion for connection.

The Psychology of Change: Turning Threats into Opportunities

From a psychological standpoint, how we interpret change directly impacts our ability to navigate it. Research on cognitive reframing reveals that viewing change as an opportunity rather than a threat activates the brain's prefrontal cortex. This brain region, responsible for decision-making and problem-solving, allows us to approach change with creativity and resilience.

On the other hand, perceiving change as a threat can trigger the amygdala, the brain's fear center, leading to stress, anxiety, and a sense of helplessness. Shifting perspective is therefore critical: when midlife changes, such as job loss, physical aging, or shifting family dynamics, are seen as invitations for growth, they can lead to unexpected and transformative outcomes.

How to Embrace Change

1. **Focus on Opportunities:** Midlife changes often create space for pursuing long-neglected interests. For instance, having more time after children leave home can allow parents to rediscover hobbies or start new projects. Similarly, a career shift may offer the freedom to explore roles more aligned with personal values.

2. **Seek Support:** Connecting with others who are undergoing similar transitions provides emotional support and practical advice. Peer groups, online forums, and professional networks can help normalize the experience of change and inspire new paths forward.

Real-Life Example: Raj's Journey of Reinvention

When Raj, a 52-year-old engineer, was downsized from his long-time corporate job, he initially felt defeated. However, after reflecting on his skills and passions, he decided to pivot into consulting. This career shift not only allowed him to continue leveraging his technical expertise but also gave him the flexibility to pursue travel, something he had dreamed about for years. By embracing change, Raj transformed a seemingly negative event into an opportunity for personal and professional fulfillment.

3. Community Engagement: Finding Purpose Through Connection

Purpose is often amplified through connection with others. Engaging in community service, volunteering, or social groups provides individuals with a sense of significance and a chance to contribute meaningfully to the world.

The Science of Altruism: A Pathway to Fulfillment

Neuroscience underscores the powerful effects of altruistic behavior. Acts of service activate the brain's reward system, including the release of oxytocin (the "bonding hormone") and dopamine (the "pleasure chemical"). These neurochemicals not only enhance mood but also foster deep social bonds and lasting memories. Engaging in purposeful activities with others reinforces our sense of belonging and validates our contributions to the greater good.

Ways to Engage

1. **Volunteer for Causes You Care About:** Whether it's mentoring at-risk youth, participating in environmental conservation, or teaching a skill, volunteering connects

individuals with meaningful work and like-minded people.

2. **Join Community Groups:** Social clubs, hobby groups, or professional organizations provide opportunities to form new relationships, exchange ideas, and collaborate on shared goals.

Real-Life Example: Ellen's Post-Retirement Transformation

After retiring, Ellen felt adrift without the daily structure of her job. She began volunteering at a local food bank, where she discovered a renewed sense of purpose through the connections she formed. Motivated by her experience, she later organized neighborhood food drives, expanding her impact, and becoming a community leader. Ellen's story illustrates how engaging with others can not only reinvigorate purpose but also spark new opportunities for leadership and collaboration.

4. Setting Realistic Goals: Progress, Not Perfection

Midlife doesn't require dramatic reinventions to be meaningful. Setting realistic, attainable goals allows individuals to build momentum, maintain focus, and foster a sense of accomplishment without overwhelming themselves.

The Neuroscience of Goal-Setting: The Power of Small Wins

Achieving even small goals activates the brain's reward system, releasing dopamine and reinforcing positive behaviors. This neurochemical response motivates individuals to continue progressing, creating a virtuous cycle of success and confidence. Conversely, setting overly ambitious or unattainable goals can lead to frustration and demotivation.

How to Set Goals

1. **Break Aspirations into Manageable Steps:** Large goals can feel daunting, but breaking them into smaller tasks makes them more achievable. For instance, someone aiming to write a novel might start by committing to writing 500 words a day.

2. **Align Goals with Current Values:** Midlife is a time to reassess priorities. Goals should reflect what truly matters, such as personal growth, family connections, or creative expression, rather than external validation like promotions or societal expectations.

Real-Life Example: David's Creative Resurgence

David, a midlife professional, always dreamed of being a writer but never pursued it seriously. He set a simple goal to write one short story a month, a manageable commitment alongside his busy schedule. This practice not only reignited his passion for storytelling but eventually led to the publication of his first book. David's journey highlights how small, realistic goals can catalyze personal transformation and fulfillment.

The Midlife Renaissance

Midlife is not an ending, it's a beginning. It is the perfect opportunity to bridge the experiences of who you've been with the aspirations of who you want to become. It's a time to reflect on the lessons learned, the paths taken, and the values cultivated, while stepping forward into a future that aligns with your evolving self. This phase invites you to embrace transformation with intention, courage, and a renewed sense of possibility.

The canvas of midlife is vast and open for reinvention. Through self-reflection, you can honor your achievements, understand what truly matters, and shed what no longer serves you. Adaptability becomes your ally as you navigate inevitable changes, transforming challenges into opportunities. By fostering deeper connections with your community and engaging in purposeful action, midlife becomes a powerful chapter of growth, meaning, and contribution.

As Carl Jung so aptly stated, "We cannot live the afternoon of life according to the program of life's morning." Midlife beckons us to reimagine purpose with the wisdom gathered from the past, the courage to embrace change, and an open heart ready to create a second act, one that is not only richer and deeper but also profoundly fulfilling in ways you may never have imagined. It's a celebration of growth, a testament to resilience, and an invitation to live authentically and purposefully.

Chapter 19

The Spiritual Journey to Purpose

Aligning the Inner Compass

Purpose often begins as a quest, a fervent chase for external markers of success, titles, accolades, and recognition. It seems natural to look outward, seeking validation and impact in the tangible world. Yet, as the layers of life unfold, a quieter truth emerges: purpose is not just about what we achieve; it's about who we are and how we connect with the world around us. It is a deeply spiritual journey, an inward exploration that aligns us with our inner compass and connects us to something far greater than ourselves.

This spiritual dimension of purpose transcends material accomplishments and touches the core of our existence. It's about finding meaning in the everyday and understanding how our lives weave into the vast tapestry of humanity and the universe. The spiritual journey to purpose invites us to pause, to look beyond the surface distractions of life, and to ask the profound questions: Why am I here? What is my role in the grander scheme of things? These questions are not mere curiosities; they are gateways to a richer, fuller understanding of life itself.

Across cultures and traditions, spirituality has served as the bridge to purpose. Ancient wisdom and modern insights converge on the idea that purpose is deeply rooted in connection, connection to oneself, to others, and to the universe.

In moments of mindfulness, faith, or universal belonging, we experience a profound sense of alignment. These moments remind us that purpose is not something we create; it's something we uncover, something that has always been within us, waiting to be realized.

Science provides intriguing insights into this connection. Neuroscience reveals that moments of spiritual reflection activate parts of the brain responsible for long-term planning, empathy, and emotional regulation. The prefrontal cortex, the temporal-parietal junction, and the reward systems all come alive, fostering clarity, compassion, and a sense of fulfillment. Psychology reinforces these findings, showing that individuals who engage in spiritual practices report higher levels of life satisfaction and resilience. This alignment with the inner compass brings coherence to life's experiences, tying them into a narrative that feels meaningful and whole.

Real-life experiences echo these truths. Consider those who find their purpose not in the grand gestures but in the quiet, intentional actions that ripple outward. A teacher who instills a love of learning in their students, a caregiver who provides comfort to the aging, or an artist who captures the beauty of fleeting moments, all of these acts stem from an alignment with the inner self. These individuals are not driven by external rewards but by a deeper calling, one that feels inseparable from who they are.

The spiritual journey to purpose also involves embracing the interconnectedness of life. When we view ourselves as part of a larger whole, our sense of purpose expands. We realize that our actions, however small, contribute to a collective reality. This understanding fosters humility and a profound sense of responsibility. It reminds us that our lives, while singular, are also shared, intertwined with the lives of others and the world at large.

Ultimately, the spiritual pursuit of purpose is not about finding definitive answers but about embracing the journey itself. It is about being present in the unfolding, recognizing the sacredness in the ordinary, and trusting that each step brings us closer to the truth of who we are meant to be. In aligning with our inner compass, we discover not just our purpose but the profound beauty of living a life of meaning and connection.

The Intersection of Spirituality and Purpose

Spirituality is not confined to religious beliefs, it encompasses a broader sense of connection, transcendence, and alignment with core values. Research in positive psychology shows that spiritual practices foster a sense of purpose by anchoring individuals in meaning, enhancing emotional resilience, and cultivating compassion. Neuroscientific studies further reveal that spiritual experiences activate the brain's reward centers, releasing dopamine and oxytocin, which enhance feelings of peace and connection.

Key Elements of the Spiritual Journey to Purpose

1. **Seeking Meaning**: At the heart of spirituality lies the pursuit of meaning, why we exist and how we fit into the larger tapestry of life. Viktor Frankl, a psychiatrist and Holocaust survivor, emphasized that meaning is central to human resilience. His groundbreaking work, *Man's Search for Meaning*, underscores that spiritual reflection provides clarity and strength during life's most challenging moments.

2. **Transcendence and Connection**: Spirituality invites us to transcend individual concerns and connect with something greater, whether it's nature, humanity, or a higher power. This transcendence fosters humility and a renewed sense of purpose by shifting focus from the self to the collective.

3. **Embracing Stillness**: Stillness, whether through meditation, prayer, or quiet reflection, creates space to tune into inner wisdom. Neuroscience demonstrates that mindfulness practices reduce activity in the default mode network (DMN), the brain's region associated with self-referential thoughts, allowing for deeper clarity and purpose.

The Intersection of Spirituality and Purpose: A Journey into Connection and Meaning

Spirituality transcends the boundaries of religious dogma; it represents a broader sense of connection, transcendence, and alignment with one's core values. It is an exploration of meaning and belonging that lies at the very heart of our existence. This universal aspect of spirituality fosters purpose by anchoring individuals in meaning, bolstering emotional resilience, and cultivating compassion.

Neuroscientific research has begun to unravel the profound effects of spiritual experiences on the brain. Spirituality activates reward centers in the brain, including the ventral striatum and the prefrontal cortex, releasing dopamine and oxytocin. Dopamine, associated with pleasure and motivation, inspires a sense of purpose, while oxytocin enhances feelings of trust, love, and connection. These chemical responses explain the inner peace and unity often reported during spiritual practices.

Key Elements of the Spiritual Journey to Purpose

Seeking Meaning

At the core of spirituality lies the pursuit of meaning, a deeply human quest to understand why we exist and how we fit into the greater tapestry of life. Viktor Frankl, a psychiatrist and Holocaust survivor, revolutionized our understanding of this through his seminal work, *Man's Search for Meaning*. He argued that meaning is not only central to human existence but also a vital source of resilience.

In neuroscience, the pursuit of meaning engages the prefrontal cortex, the brain's executive center responsible for planning and complex decision-making. This region helps individuals piece together their experiences into a coherent life narrative. For laypeople, this means that when we reflect on why certain experiences matter, be it helping a loved one, pursuing a passion, or facing adversity, we activate the very mechanisms that enhance resilience and focus.

Consider someone facing a midlife career change. By seeking meaning in their journey, they might recognize their true calling is to mentor others rather than climb the corporate ladder. This shift in perspective fosters renewed purpose, as they align their goals with their deeper values.

Transcendence and Connection

Spirituality invites us to look beyond ourselves, fostering a sense of transcendence that connects us to something larger, nature, humanity, or a higher power. This shift from self-centric concerns to collective awareness brings humility and a renewed sense of purpose.

From a neurological standpoint, transcendence is associated with decreased activity in the brain's default mode network (DMN), which is responsible for self-referential thinking. By quieting the DMN, spiritual practices such as prayer, meditation, or even spending time in nature allow individuals to step out of their egos and perceive the interconnectedness of life. This connection to a larger whole fosters empathy and compassion, traits essential for purposeful living.

For example, imagine a community volunteer who dedicates their weekends to cleaning up public spaces. The act itself transcends individual gain, connecting them to their environment and their community. Over time, this alignment with a greater cause nurtures a profound sense of purpose.

Embracing Stillness

Stillness is an essential yet often overlooked aspect of the spiritual journey. In our hyper-connected world, taking time for quiet reflection creates the mental space needed to tune into inner wisdom. Practices like meditation, prayer, and silent walks are all avenues to stillness that foster purpose.

Neuroscience has shown that mindfulness practices reduce activity in the DMN, decreasing the mind's tendency to ruminate on negative or self-focused thoughts. This allows for deeper clarity and insight. In layman's terms, stillness acts like a mental reset button, clearing away the noise of daily stress to reveal what truly matters.

Consider a person overwhelmed by life's demands. When they set aside 15 minutes daily for meditation or journaling, they create a space to listen to their inner voice. Over time, this practice can reveal patterns, desires, or values they were previously too distracted to notice, paving the way for a more purpose-driven life.

A Science-Backed Human Experience

Spirituality and purpose form a dynamic interplay that is deeply embedded in the human experience. Together, they create a feedback loop that enriches our lives, anchoring us in meaning while fostering deeper connections with ourselves, others, and the world. This connection is not merely philosophical or anecdotal; it is rooted in the intricate workings of the brain and validated by psychological studies. This science-backed perspective reveals how spirituality and purpose act as catalysts for a more fulfilling and aligned existence.

Neurobiology of Meaning and Reward

The pursuit of meaning, the cornerstone of both spirituality and purpose, activates key brain regions involved in planning, decision-making, and reward processing. Specifically, the prefrontal cortex, which governs long-term thinking and goal-setting, collaborates with the ventral striatum, the brain's reward center, to generate a sense of satisfaction and motivation.

When individuals engage in activities aligned with their values or life goals, such as volunteering, creating art, or practicing mindfulness, these regions light up with activity. This neural activation explains why living with purpose feels rewarding and motivating: the brain is wired to associate meaningful pursuits with pleasure and fulfillment. In practical terms, this means that purpose-driven actions, even small ones, can help combat feelings of stagnation or aimlessness by stimulating the brain's natural reward pathways.

For example, consider someone who mentors a younger colleague at work. Although this action may seem minor, it taps into their core values of teaching and contributing to others' growth. The resulting sense of satisfaction stems from this alignment, fueled by the brain's neurochemical response.

Transcendence and the Reduction of Self-Focus

One of spirituality's profound effects is its ability to transcend the self, fostering a sense of connection to something greater, be it a higher power, nature, or the collective human experience. This transcendence is not just an abstract concept; it is a measurable phenomenon in the brain.

Research into mindfulness and spiritual practices shows that they deactivate the brain's default mode network (DMN), which is responsible for self-referential thinking. The DMN is often active when we ruminate on personal concerns or dwell on past regrets and future anxieties. By quieting the DMN, spiritual practices reduce self-focus and enable individuals to shift their attention outward. This creates space for empathy, humility, and a broader perspective on life.

In human terms, transcendence often manifests in moments of awe, standing at the edge of the ocean, gazing at the stars, or connecting deeply with another person. These moments remind us of our small yet meaningful place in the vastness of existence, helping to recalibrate priorities and reinforce purpose.

For example, a teacher who spends a weekend volunteering for environmental conservation might experience a deep connection to nature. This connection may inspire a renewed commitment to incorporating sustainability into their curriculum, reflecting the ripple effect of purpose beyond themselves.

Stillness and Inner Clarity

In the fast-paced modern world, stillness is a luxury few indulge in, yet it is a cornerstone of the spiritual journey and its connection to purpose. Neuroscientific studies reveal that practices like meditation, prayer, or deep reflection reduce activity in the amygdala, the brain's fear, and emotion center, while increasing connectivity between the prefrontal cortex and the hippocampus. This shift promotes clarity, reduces stress, and enhances memory and focus.

For individuals, stillness creates the mental space necessary to reflect on what truly matters. It allows for the integration of experiences, helping people identify patterns, desires, or values that might otherwise remain obscured by the noise of daily life. In simpler terms, taking time to pause and reflect enables us to listen to our inner compass, a key step in aligning actions with purpose.

Consider the story of a business professional who, amidst the chaos of work and family life, commits to daily mindfulness practice. Through stillness, they begin to realize that their true passion lies in mentoring young entrepreneurs rather than pursuing personal career accolades. This clarity leads them to realign their professional path with their deeper purpose, fostering fulfillment and growth.

Tangible and Intangible Enrichment

The intertwining of spirituality and purpose offers benefits that are both tangible and intangible. On a tangible level, people who engage with spiritual practices and purpose-driven activities often experience lower stress levels, improved physical health, and stronger social connections. These outcomes are supported by reduced cortisol levels, enhanced cardiovascular health, and the neurochemical rewards of oxytocin and dopamine.

Intangibly, the effects are equally profound. Spirituality and purpose foster a sense of coherence, helping individuals weave together disparate life experiences into a meaningful narrative. They enhance emotional resilience, enabling people to navigate challenges with grace and optimism. Most importantly, they cultivate a sense of belonging, reminding us that we are part of a larger story.

For instance, a retiree who begins teaching art classes at a local community center may find joy in the tangible benefits of reduced isolation and improved health. Yet, the intangible rewards, watching students grow, rediscovering their own creativity, and contributing to the community, are what truly enrich their soul.

The Unified Experience

The intersection of spirituality and purpose creates a unified experience that integrates mind, body, and spirit. This alignment allows individuals to move through life with a sense of direction and peace, regardless of external circumstances. Whether through small daily practices like gratitude journaling or life-altering commitments like pursuing a new career aligned with one's values, the combined power of spirituality and purpose offers a pathway to a richer, more connected existence.

At its core, this journey is not about achieving perfection but about embracing the continuous evolution of self. By understanding the science and embracing the lived experience of this intersection, individuals can unlock the transformative potential of purpose as both a deeply personal and universally shared human endeavor.

The Spiritual Practices That Foster Purpose

Spiritual practices serve as pathways to deepen our connection with purpose, providing structure and intention to align with our core values. These practices, rooted in both tradition and modern science, offer tangible and transformative tools for cultivating a meaningful life. Let's delve into each practice and its unique contribution to fostering purpose.

1. Mindfulness and Meditation

Mindfulness and meditation are foundational practices for aligning with purpose. By fostering presence and reducing distractions, they enable a deeper awareness of what truly matters. These practices are scientifically proven to calm the mind and promote emotional resilience, creating the mental space needed for introspection.

A 2020 study published in *Frontiers in Psychology* found that regular meditation strengthens the connection between the prefrontal cortex (responsible for decision-making and long-term thinking) and the amygdala (the brain's fear and emotion center). This enhanced connection fosters emotional balance and clarity, helping individuals prioritize purpose-driven actions over reactive impulses.

- **Practical Tip:** Start with a simple 10-minute daily meditation. Focus on your breath or engage in guided visualizations that center on your purpose. For instance, imagine yourself contributing positively to the lives of others or achieving a goal aligned with your core values.

- **Layman's Perspective:** Imagine your mind as a cluttered desk. Meditation is like organizing that desk, clearing away distractions so you can focus on what's truly important. By practicing mindfulness, you can better recognize opportunities to live with intention.

2. Journaling for Reflection

Journaling offers a space for spiritual inquiry and self-discovery. Writing down thoughts and emotions allows individuals to process experiences, identify patterns, and connect with their innermost values. It is particularly effective in fostering clarity of purpose by externalizing internal questions and reflections.

Prompts like *"What gives my life meaning?"* or *"How do I want to be remembered?"* encourage deep exploration and provide a roadmap for purpose-driven decisions. Journaling also activates the brain's prefrontal cortex, enhancing cognitive processing and emotional regulation.

- **Real-Life Example:** Maya, a corporate executive, used journaling to navigate her midlife transition. Through reflective prompts, she discovered a passion for mentoring young professionals. This realization led her to shift her career focus, aligning her work with her desire to make a difference.

- **Layman's Perspective:** Think of journaling as a mirror for your thoughts. It helps you see your inner self more clearly, highlighting what truly brings you joy and fulfillment. Writing out your thoughts can reveal unexpected insights, just as Maya discovered her passion for mentoring.

3. Engaging in Rituals

Rituals, whether rooted in tradition or personal practice, ground individuals in routine and intentionality. They create moments of predictability that reduce anxiety and foster a sense of control. Whether lighting a candle, practicing yoga, or participating in religious ceremonies, rituals provide a sense of connection to the sacred and the purposeful.

From a scientific perspective, rituals activate the brain's reward pathways, releasing dopamine, which promotes a sense of accomplishment and peace. They also reduce activity in the brain's stress centers, offering a calming effect that supports introspection and alignment with purpose.

- **Scientific Perspective:** Rituals, even simple ones, create neural associations with stability and meaning. For example, lighting a candle every evening as a symbol of gratitude for the day can reinforce a mindset of appreciation and purpose.

- **Layman's Perspective:** Think of rituals as anchors in a stormy sea. They provide stability and a sense of grounding, helping you focus on what matters most. Even small acts, like pausing for a moment of gratitude each morning, can bring you closer to your purpose.

4. Acts of Service

Serving others is one of the most profound ways to foster purpose. Altruism, whether through volunteering, mentoring, or supporting a loved one, activates the brain's reward system, releasing oxytocin and dopamine. These neurochemicals enhance mood, deepen social bonds, and create lasting feelings of fulfillment.

Acts of service also shift the focus from self-centered concerns to the collective good. This shift aligns with the spiritual principle of interconnectedness, reinforcing the idea that we are part of something greater than ourselves.

- **Real-Life Example:** John, a retired teacher, found new meaning in life by tutoring underserved children in his community. What began as a small act of kindness blossomed into a fulfilling journey of connection and impact. Through service, John experienced not only the joy of helping others but also a renewed sense of his own purpose.

- **Layman's Perspective:** Imagine planting a tree in a barren field. While it benefits the environment, it also brings joy and a sense of accomplishment to the planter. Acts of service are like planting those trees in the lives of others, they grow into something far greater than the initial act.

The Unified Power of Spiritual Practices

Each of these practices, mindfulness, journaling, rituals, and service, offers a unique pathway to connect with purpose. Together, they form a holistic approach to aligning with our values and transcending the distractions of daily life. By integrating these practices into your routine, you not only foster a deeper sense of purpose but also create ripples of positive change that extend to your community and beyond.

The Transformative Power of Spiritual Purpose

Spiritual purpose possesses a profound ability to reshape not only individuals but also the communities they touch. It anchors us in meaning, serving as a guiding force that inspires positive change, fosters resilience, and nurtures compassion. Rooted in our shared humanity, spiritual purpose transcends personal goals, creating a ripple effect that connects us to something greater than ourselves. This transformative power is both deeply personal and universally impactful.

Anchoring oneself in spiritual purpose is akin to planting a tree with deep roots, steadying us during life's storms while allowing our influence to branch out and touch others. Through this connection to purpose, we find clarity and direction, becoming catalysts for change in our personal lives, relationships, and communities. When individuals operate from a place of spiritual alignment, they embody qualities like empathy, courage, and hope, which radiate outward and inspire others.

The spiritual journey to purpose is not a straight line; it's a dynamic and ever-evolving exploration. Life's uncertainties and challenges act as both obstacles and opportunities, pushing us to reevaluate, reflect, and reconnect with our innermost values. This cyclical process of discovery deepens our understanding of ourselves and our place in the world, nurturing a sense of fulfillment that cannot be derived from external accomplishments alone.

Neuroscience reveals that this connection to purpose has tangible effects on our minds and bodies. The pursuit of spiritual purpose activates brain regions associated with reward, motivation, and emotional regulation, such as the ventral striatum and prefrontal cortex. These neural pathways strengthen our ability to cope with stress, sustain hope, and cultivate emotional resilience. At the same time, the release of neurochemicals like oxytocin and dopamine fosters feelings of connection and joy, reinforcing the bonds we form with others along the journey.

For communities, the transformative power of spiritual purpose lies in its capacity to unite and inspire collective action. History is filled with examples of movements rooted in spiritual ideals, moments where shared purpose transcended individual differences to create profound social change. Whether through grassroots activism, acts of service, or shared rituals, these collective efforts demonstrate the immense potential of spiritual purpose to foster collaboration and solidarity.

This chapter has delved into the intersection of spirituality and purpose, weaving together insights from science, real-life stories, and practical tools. It underscores that spirituality, whether expressed through quiet introspection, communal engagement, or acts of kindness, serves as a beacon that guides us toward a meaningful life.

The journey inward illuminates the path outward, reminding us that purpose is not a solitary pursuit but a shared experience that connects us all. By embracing this transformative power, we not only enrich our own lives but also contribute to a world that thrives on compassion, connection, and hope.

Chapter 20

Transcending Materialism

In a world driven by consumerism, material wealth is often mistaken for success and fulfillment. Yet, as countless studies and personal stories reveal, the relentless pursuit of materialism often leaves us feeling empty, disconnected, and yearning for something deeper. Transcending materialism is not about rejecting the material world entirely but about reorienting our values, finding meaning beyond possessions, and embracing a purpose-driven life that fulfills both the soul and the mind.

The Illusion of Fulfillment in Materialism

The human brain is wired to seek rewards, a function rooted in the dopaminergic system. Buying a new car, a bigger house, or the latest gadget activates this system, releasing dopamine and providing a fleeting sense of pleasure. However, research consistently shows that the satisfaction derived from material acquisitions is short-lived. This phenomenon, known as the **hedonic treadmill**, explains why people quickly adapt to their new possessions and begin craving the next "bigger and better" thing.

While material gains can provide comfort and security, they often fail to address deeper emotional and psychological needs. Neuroscience highlights that activities rooted in meaning and purpose, rather than material rewards, stimulate the brain's **default mode network** (DMN), fostering reflection, connection, and long-term satisfaction. In contrast, the ceaseless pursuit of materialism keeps the brain in a cycle of external validation, preventing introspection and personal growth.

The Neuroscience of Purpose Over Possessions

Purposeful living offers a stark contrast to materialistic pursuits. Studies reveal that engaging in activities that align with personal values, such as volunteering, creative expression, or nurturing relationships, activates the brain's **ventromedial prefrontal cortex** (vmPFC), a region associated with meaning, reward, and long-term planning. Unlike material rewards, which spark transient dopamine spikes, purpose-driven actions create enduring feelings of fulfillment by integrating emotional and cognitive satisfaction.

Additionally, **oxytocin**, the "bonding hormone," plays a critical role in fostering happiness through connections rather than possessions. Acts of kindness, community engagement, and deep conversations stimulate oxytocin release, reinforcing feelings of trust, belonging, and purpose. Neuroscience thus underscores that true contentment stems from meaningful experiences and relationships, not material accumulation.

The Psychological Cost of Materialism

The psychological toll of materialism cannot be overlooked. Research has linked materialistic values to increased levels of anxiety, depression, and low self-esteem. Psychologist Tim Kasser, in his seminal work *The High Price of Materialism*, found that individuals who prioritize wealth, image, and status often experience diminished well-being and strained relationships. This occurs because materialism diverts attention from intrinsic goals, like personal growth, connection, and community, that are essential for mental health.

Moreover, the constant comparison inherent in materialistic pursuits exacerbates feelings of inadequacy. Social media platforms amplify this effect, showcasing curated images of wealth and success that fuel envy and dissatisfaction. The brain's **anterior cingulate cortex** (ACC), responsible for processing social comparison, becomes hyperactive in such scenarios, leading to increased stress and emotional turbulence. Breaking free from this cycle requires a conscious shift in focus from "having more" to "being more."

Transcending Materialism: A Pathway to Freedom

Transcending materialism is not about renouncing all possessions but about redefining their role in our lives. It involves shifting from a mindset of accumulation to one of contribution, from seeking external validation to cultivating internal fulfillment.

1. **Cultivating Gratitude** Gratitude rewires the brain to focus on abundance rather than scarcity. Studies using functional MRI (fMRI) scans show that practicing gratitude activates the **medial prefrontal cortex**, enhancing emotional regulation and reducing the desire for material rewards. By appreciating what we already have, we break the cycle of constant wanting and foster contentment.

    - **Practical Exercise**: Begin a daily gratitude journal. Write down three things you're grateful for, focusing on relationships, experiences, or personal growth rather than possessions.

2. **Prioritizing Experiences Over Possessions** Research consistently shows that spending money on experiences, like travel, concerts, or learning new skills, brings more

lasting happiness than buying material goods. Experiences create memories and strengthen connections, engaging the brain's **hippocampus** and fostering a sense of identity and belonging.

- **Real-Life Perspective**: Instead of buying the latest smartphone, consider investing in a weekend getaway with loved ones. The joy derived from shared experiences often outweighs the fleeting pleasure of new gadgets.

3. **Fostering Relationships** Strong relationships are a cornerstone of transcending materialism. Neuroscience reveals that social connections release oxytocin and endorphins, enhancing happiness and resilience. By investing time and energy in meaningful relationships, we cultivate a support system that enriches our lives far beyond what material possessions can offer.

    - **Tip for Practice**: Dedicate regular time to nurture relationships. Host family dinners, schedule calls with friends, or volunteer in community groups to build deeper connections.

4. **Engaging in Purpose-Driven Actions** Purposeful activities shift focus from "what can I gain?" to "how can I give?" Acts of service and altruism not only benefit others but also bring profound joy to the giver. Neuroscientific studies demonstrate that altruistic actions activate the brain's reward centers more effectively than self-centered pursuits.

    - **Real-Life Example**: Consider John, a retired banker who found fulfillment by mentoring young entrepreneurs. By sharing his knowledge, he experienced a renewed sense of purpose and witnessed the ripple effect of his contributions.

5. **Mindfulness and Simplification** Simplifying life and practicing mindfulness allows us to disengage from the constant noise of consumerism. Mindfulness practices reduce activity in the **amygdala**, the brain's fear center, promoting calm and clarity. Simplifying our surroundings and commitments creates mental space for self-reflection and intentional living.

- **Action Step**: Adopt a "one in, one out" rule for possessions. For every new item you acquire, donate, or discard an old one. This practice encourages mindful consumption and reduces clutter.

The Ripple Effect of Transcending Materialism

Transcending materialism doesn't just transform individuals, it impacts communities and society at large. When we prioritize purpose over possessions, we model values that inspire others to do the same. Families become more connected, workplaces more collaborative, and communities more compassionate. On a global scale, movements toward sustainability and ethical consumption demonstrate how collective shifts in values can create a more equitable and harmonious world.

Consider the example of Patagonia, a company that has built its brand on purpose rather than profit. By prioritizing environmental sustainability and ethical practices, Patagonia has not only achieved business success but has also inspired industry-wide changes in corporate responsibility.

Embracing the Journey

Transcending materialism is a lifelong journey, not a destination. It requires intentionality, reflection, and a commitment to values that nourish the soul rather than fleeting desires. It invites us to ask: What truly matters? What legacy do we want to leave? These questions guide us toward a life that prioritizes meaning, connection, and purpose.

As we close this chapter, consider the words of Mahatma Gandhi: "You may never know what results come of your actions, but if you do nothing, there will be no result." By transcending materialism, we not only reclaim our personal freedom but also contribute to a world driven by purpose, compassion, and shared humanity.

Chapter 21

Redefining Work and Success

Success has traditionally been defined by metrics that are easily quantifiable, wealth, titles, accolades, or even the size of one's office. Yet, as societies evolve and individual aspirations shift, it has become clear that these conventional measures often fail to capture what truly matters. Work is no longer just about productivity or financial gain; it is increasingly being seen as a reflection of purpose, values, and identity.

To redefine work and success, we must confront deeply ingrained myths, question outdated frameworks, and adopt a more intentional, holistic perspective. This part of the book explores how individuals and organizations can move beyond superficial metrics to embrace a deeper, more meaningful understanding of achievement.

The Problem with Traditional Metrics of Success

The industrial age solidified the idea that work and success are transactional: the more hours you put in, the more rewards you reap. This mindset has persisted for decades, yet it fails to account for the human desire for fulfillment, purpose, and balance.

Historically, even the most accomplished individuals have questioned the value of their success when disconnected from purpose. Consider the life of **Andrew Carnegie**, one of the wealthiest men of his era. Despite his immense financial success,

Carnegie grappled with a deep sense of responsibility, eventually channeling his fortune into philanthropic efforts, famously stating, "The man who dies rich dies disgraced." His realization underscores a truth that resonates across time: success without purpose is ultimately hollow.

In the modern world, burnout, disengagement, and dissatisfaction are symptoms of this misalignment. A 2023 **Gallup poll** found that only 21% of employees globally feel engaged at work, despite rising incomes and advancements in workplace conditions. This disconnect suggests that traditional success metrics are no longer sufficient to sustain motivation or fulfillment.

Rethinking Success: Beyond Wealth and Status

To redefine success, we need a paradigm shift from accumulation to alignment. Success should reflect who you are, not just what you have achieved. This shift requires considering several dimensions:

1. **Purpose**: Success should be aligned with one's core values and aspirations. Work that resonates with your purpose is intrinsically rewarding, creating a sense of accomplishment that transcends external recognition.

2. **Impact**: True success considers the impact you have on others, whether through mentorship, innovation, or social contributions. Companies like **Patagonia**, which prioritizes environmental sustainability, demonstrate how impact-driven work can redefine organizational success.

3. **Balance**: The notion of success should incorporate balance between work and life. People like **Warren Buffett**, who famously schedules time for reading and

reflection, exemplify how balance fosters long-term fulfillment and creativity.

4. **Growth**: Success should reflect personal and professional growth, emphasizing learning, adaptability, and the ability to navigate challenges. Thomas Edison's reframing of thousands of failed experiments as steps toward success illustrates this perspective.

Redefining Work: From Tasks to Meaning

Redefining success also requires rethinking work itself. Work should not just be a series of tasks or obligations; it should be a meaningful pursuit that aligns with individual and collective purpose.

- **The Evolution of Work**: Historically, work has transitioned from subsistence farming to industrialized labor, and now to knowledge and purpose-driven economies. Each stage has brought new definitions of what work entails. In today's context, work should be seen as a vehicle for expression, innovation, and contribution.

- **The Role of Organizations**: Companies play a critical role in redefining work. Organizations that prioritize purpose alongside profit, like Tesla's mission to accelerate sustainable energy, attract employees and customers who share their vision. This alignment fosters loyalty, innovation, and long-term success.

Practical Frameworks for Redefining Work and Success

1. The Triple Bottom Line

The **Triple Bottom Line Framework** evaluates success through three dimensions: **Profit, People, and Planet**. It challenges organizations to consider financial performance alongside social and environmental impact.

- **Application**: When setting professional goals, evaluate how your work contributes not only to personal achievement but also to broader societal or environmental outcomes.

2. Ikigai

The Japanese concept of Ikigai, meaning "reason for being," combines four elements: What you love, what you're good at, what the world needs, and what you can be paid for.

- **Application**: Reflect on how your current work aligns with these dimensions. Where gaps exist, consider steps to bring them into alignment, such as exploring roles or projects that fulfill multiple dimensions of Ikigai.

3. Agile Work Principles

Borrowed from software development, **Agile principles** emphasize flexibility, collaboration, and continuous improvement. Applying these principles to career development can help individuals and teams adapt to changing circumstances while staying aligned with purpose.

- **Application**: Periodically assess your work goals and practices. Are they still serving your purpose? If not, iterate and adjust, just as Agile teams adapt their workflows.

The Science of Meaningful Work

Neuroscience reveals that work tied to purpose activates the brain's reward system, particularly through the release of dopamine. This reinforces motivation and satisfaction. In contrast, work that feels disconnected or meaningless can trigger stress responses, leading to disengagement and burnout.

Historical examples further illustrate this dynamic. **Leonardo da Vinci**, for instance, derived immense satisfaction from work that combined his passions for art and science. His ability to find meaning in his pursuits allowed him to remain engaged and innovative, leaving a legacy that continues to inspire.

Steps to Redefine Your Work and Success

1. **Revisit Your Definition of Success:**
    - Write down what success means to you. Compare it to societal definitions. Where do they diverge, and how can you align your actions with your personal definition?

2. **Integrate Purpose into Daily Work:**
    - Identify one task or project each day that resonates with your values. Focus on how it contributes to your sense of purpose.

3. **Evaluate Impact Regularly:**
    - Reflect on how your work benefits others, whether it's your team, community, or a broader audience.

Celebrate moments when you've made a positive difference.

4. **Adopt a Growth Mindset:**
   - View challenges as opportunities to grow rather than obstacles to success. Seek out learning experiences that push you outside your comfort zone.

5. **Balance Achievement with Fulfillment:**
   - Create boundaries that protect time for rest, hobbies, and relationships. Fulfillment comes not from constant striving but from harmonizing work with other aspects of life.

A New Lens on Work and Success

Redefining work and success are not about rejecting traditional metrics entirely; it's about integrating them with deeper, more meaningful dimensions. It's about moving beyond the superficial chase for status or wealth and embracing a holistic view that values purpose, impact, growth, and balance.

This redefinition is not a one-time effort; it's an ongoing journey. Like Andrew Carnegie's shift from wealth accumulation to philanthropy, or Leonardo da Vinci's seamless integration of art and science, it requires constant reflection and recalibration.

As you redefine what success means for you, remember that the ultimate measure of success isn't found in titles or trophies but in the alignment of your work with your values and the positive impact you leave behind. In doing so, you'll discover that success isn't something to chase, it's something to live.

Moving Beyond the Paycheck and Building Your Purpose Legacy

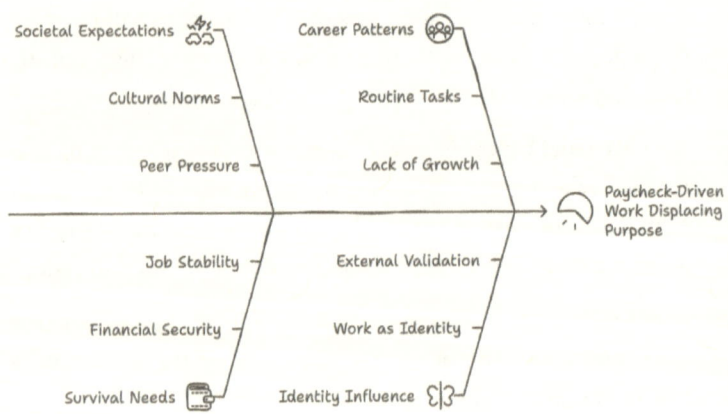

From Paycheck to Purpose: A Path to Fulfillment

In the hustle of modern life, the paycheck often becomes the North Star. It's tangible, measurable, and dependable, an anchor in a world of uncertainties. But as years roll by, you might find yourself wondering: is this all there is? Is work just a trade of hours for money, a ceaseless cycle of effort that deposits funds into your bank account but leaves your soul running on empty?

The reality is stark yet universal: many of us fall into the trap of paycheck-driven work. It's not a conscious choice, it's survival, a societal expectation, a default mode that shapes careers, relationships, and identities. The irony, however, is that the paycheck, as necessary as it is, is also the greatest distraction from what truly matters: purpose, fulfillment, and legacy.

The Allure of the Paycheck

Imagine a young professional, let's call him Arjun. Fresh out of college, Arjun lands his first corporate job. His friends envy his paycheck, it's more than they ever imagined earning at this stage of life. His family is proud, his LinkedIn profile gleams with congratulatory messages, and Arjun feels like he's finally "made it."

At first, the paycheck feels like validation. It allows him to buy the things he's always wanted, plan vacations, and indulge in a lifestyle he once aspired to. But over time, something shifts. Each raise, each bonus, starts to feel less like a reward and more like a pacifier. The thrill wanes, replaced by a gnawing question: "Why doesn't this feel as good as it should?"

Arjun's story is not unique. It's the story of countless professionals who discover that money, while necessary, is not sufficient to sustain a sense of fulfillment. The cycle of working for the next paycheck becomes a golden cage, a trap that blinds people to the possibilities of a richer, more meaningful existence.

The Historical Roots of Paycheck Mentality

To understand why this mindset persists, we need to step back in time. The industrial revolution in the 18th and 19th centuries fundamentally reshaped the way people thought about work. Factories required disciplined, time-bound labor, and wages became the primary measure of a worker's value. The rise of capitalism further entrenched this idea, linking human worth to productivity and financial output.

The legacy of this era still lingers. Today, job titles and salaries serve as social currency. Ask someone what they do, and their response will often center on their role or income bracket rather than their passions or impact. It's no wonder that the paycheck dominates our collective psyche, it has been hardwired into the cultural narrative for centuries.

But history also offers a counterpoint. Consider **Mahatma Gandhi**, who renounced material wealth to pursue a life of service and purpose. Gandhi's decision wasn't just philosophical; it was deeply practical. He believed that true fulfillment came not from accumulation but from alignment with one's values. His life stands as a testament to the idea that moving beyond the paycheck doesn't mean abandoning it entirely, it means reframing it as a tool, not a goal.

The Psychological Cost of Paycheck Dependency

Relying solely on a paycheck for fulfillment has psychological consequences. Studies have shown that individuals who view work purely as a means to an end are more likely to experience burnout, disengagement, and dissatisfaction. The concept of **extrinsic motivation**, where actions are driven by external rewards like money, often leads to diminishing returns. Over time, the reward loses its luster, and the work becomes a chore.

Contrast this with **intrinsic motivation**, where actions are driven by internal satisfaction. People who find meaning in their work, be it solving problems, helping others, or creating something new, report higher levels of happiness and resilience. The paycheck becomes a byproduct, not the purpose.

Neuroscience supports this distinction. When work aligns with intrinsic motivation, the brain's **reward system** releases dopamine, creating a sense of pleasure and accomplishment. In contrast, paycheck-driven work activates the brain's stress response, particularly when the rewards feel disconnected from personal values or aspirations.

Moving Beyond the Paycheck: A Paradigm Shift

Moving beyond the paycheck doesn't mean rejecting financial goals, it means broadening your definition of success. Here's how:

1. **Reframe Work as Contribution:**
   - Instead of viewing work solely as a source of income, ask yourself: What am I contributing? Whether it's innovation, support, or inspiration, focusing on contribution shifts the narrative from taking to giving.

- **Example**: Consider the story of **Elon Musk**, whose work with Tesla and SpaceX isn't just about profits but about transforming transportation and space exploration. His paycheck is a side effect of his commitment to larger goals.

2. **Connect Work to Values:**
   - Aligning your daily tasks with your core values fosters a sense of meaning. If your work feels disconnected, seek opportunities to infuse it with purpose. Volunteer for projects that excite you, mentor younger colleagues, or advocate for causes that resonate with you.

3. **Prioritize Experiences Over Accumulation:**
   - Research shows that experiences, not material possessions, are what bring lasting happiness. Use your paycheck as a means to enrich your life through travel, learning, or quality time with loved ones.

4. **Set Impactful Goals:**
   - Shift your goals from "earning X amount" to "creating X impact." This subtle change reorients your efforts toward purpose-driven outcomes.

Stories of Those Who Transcended

History is replete with individuals who moved beyond the paycheck to find deeper fulfillment.

- **John D. Rockefeller**, one of the richest men in history, eventually turned his focus to philanthropy, founding institutions that transformed healthcare and education. His purpose expanded beyond wealth accumulation to societal betterment.

- **Oprah Winfrey**, despite immense financial success, often speaks about her work's purpose: inspiring and empowering others. Her paycheck is substantial, but her drive comes from connecting with people and making a difference.

- **Muhammad Yunus**, founder of Grameen Bank, revolutionized microfinance by prioritizing the economic empowerment of the poor. His work transcended personal gain, focusing instead on systemic change.

Practical Steps to Move Beyond the Paycheck

1. **Redefine Success:**
   - Write down your definition of success. Does it include meaningful work, relationships, or impact? Compare this with how you currently spend your time and energy.

2. **Create Purposeful Rituals:**
   - Start your workday by identifying one task that aligns with your values. End it by reflecting on how your efforts contributed to something larger.

3. **Build a Vision Beyond Work:**
   - Develop a personal mission statement that encompasses your aspirations outside of your career. Let this vision guide your decisions.

4. **Seek Growth Opportunities:**
   - Pursue roles or projects that challenge you to grow. Growth fuels engagement, making work more than just a paycheck.

5. **Embrace Financial Stewardship:**
   - Use your paycheck wisely to support your purpose. Invest in causes, education, or experiences that enrich your life and align with your values.

Your purpose legacy is not the sum of your titles, the awards on your mantel, or the zeros in your bank account. It is the imprint you leave behind, the invisible thread that ties your life to the lives of others in ways that transcend time. It's the answer to a question far more profound than "What do you do?" it's the answer to "Why does your life matter?"

A legacy isn't born in moments of grandeur. It's shaped in the quiet choices you make daily, in how you treat others, in the courage you summon to align your actions with your values, and in the risks, you take to pursue what feels right rather than what feels easy. Your legacy begins when you stop chasing validation and start building something that reflects who you are, something that will continue to resonate long after you've gone.

Defining Legacy in a Noisy World

We live in a world obsessed with fleeting markers of success. Social media bombards us with highlight reels of achievement, turning life into a relentless competition for visibility. In this environment, legacy can feel like an abstract, distant concept. But your legacy isn't about trending hashtags or temporary applause. It's about the quiet, persistent impact you leave on the lives you touch and the causes you champion.

Consider **Steve Jobs**, a figure often remembered for his genius in revolutionizing technology. Yet, Jobs's legacy wasn't just the iPhone or the MacBook, it was his relentless pursuit of excellence and his vision of creating tools that empower people to unleash their creativity. Jobs didn't merely build products; he built a philosophy that still inspires innovation today. His legacy wasn't in the profits he earned but in the possibilities he unlocked.

Why Legacy Matters

Your purpose legacy matters because it shifts the focus of your life from accumulation to contribution. It forces you to ask, "What will endure?" and compels you to live with intention. A paycheck might sustain you, but a legacy sustains others. It lives on in the knowledge you pass down, the systems you challenge, the communities you uplift, and the moments when your presence made a difference.

But legacy isn't just about grand achievements. It's also about the small, everyday choices that align with your values. It's in the teacher who inspires students to believe in themselves, the entrepreneur who builds a business rooted in ethical practices, the parent who models integrity for their children. Legacy is lived in the quiet but profound moments when your actions ripple outward in ways you may never fully see.

Building Your Purpose Legacy

To build a purpose legacy, you must first embrace the idea that it's not something you leave behind, it's something you cultivate every day. It's not a monument you construct at the end of your life but a garden you tend throughout it. Here's how:

1. **Clarify Your Values**: Your legacy begins with knowing what you stand for. Reflect on the principles that matter most to you, whether it's integrity, creativity, compassion, or justice. These values will serve as the foundation for your legacy.

2. **Take Meaningful Action**: A legacy isn't built on intentions alone. It's forged through deliberate action. Look for ways to live your values through your work, relationships, and contributions to society. It might be as simple as mentoring a colleague or as ambitious as launching a movement.

3. **Focus on Impact, Not Recognition**: Legacy isn't about being remembered; it's about making a difference. Shift your focus from seeking accolades to creating impact. The most enduring legacies often come from people who worked quietly but powerfully to improve the world around them.

4. **Invest in People**: Your legacy isn't just what you achieve; it's who you help. Pour your energy into building others up, teaching, guiding, and empowering them to carry your values forward. A legacy is amplified when it lives on in the hearts and minds of others.

5. **Redefine Success**: Success and legacy aren't the same. While success is often individual and immediate, legacy is collective and enduring. Redefine success as the alignment of your work with your purpose, the positive impact you have on others, and the fulfillment you find in living authentically.

Living Your Legacy Now

The most powerful legacies aren't reserved for the future; they are lived in the present. Legacy isn't about waiting for the perfect moment or accumulating enough resources, it's about acting with purpose today. When you bring intention to your daily actions, when you treat your work as a means to contribute rather than just earn, you're already building your legacy.

Look to someone like **Maya Angelou**, whose words and actions during her lifetime elevated countless others. Angelou's poetry and activism weren't designed to immortalize her name but to give voice to those who had been silenced. Her legacy isn't confined to history books, it lives in the millions who continue to draw strength from her words.

Your Call to Action

Ask yourself this: If your life were a book, what would the final chapter say? Would it be a story of chasing temporary rewards, or would it be a testament to the difference you made? Moving beyond the paycheck and into your purpose legacy isn't an abstract ideal, it's a choice. A choice to live with intention, to align your actions with your values, and to prioritize impact over applause.

Your legacy is being written every day. It's in the risks you take, the lives you touch, and the courage you show in living authentically. It's not just the story of your work but the story of your life, a story that, if told well, will inspire others to do the same.

So, step forward. Live not just for the paycheck but for the legacy that will endure long after it. Write your chapter with care, for it's a gift to the world, and it's uniquely yours to give.

The Journey Ahead: Building an Intentional Career backed by Purpose

As we reach the conclusion of this exploration, it's clear that the journey beyond the paycheck is not a rejection of financial goals but a reimagining of them. In a world where work often defines identity, transcending the confines of a paycheck means redefining success as something far greater than monetary gain. It's about understanding that while financial stability is a foundation, true fulfillment comes from aligning work with meaning, impact, and purpose.

The Shift in Perspective

For generations, the paycheck has been the ultimate metric of success. But as we've seen through history, psychology, and neuroscience, the most fulfilled individuals are those who move beyond this singular focus. Figures like Mahatma Gandhi, who dedicated his life to service, or Oprah Winfrey, who built a legacy of empowerment and storytelling, remind us that true success lies in living a life of purpose.

The science supports this shift. Studies reveal that intrinsic rewards, those rooted in personal growth, connection, and contribution, stimulate long-term satisfaction more effectively than extrinsic ones like wealth or status. The brain's reward centers, including the **ventral striatum**, respond more robustly to acts of altruism and personal fulfillment than to fleeting material gains. This is a testament to humanity's innate drive to create meaning and make a difference.

The Ongoing Process of Reflection and Alignment

Moving beyond the paycheck isn't a one-time decision; it's a lifelong journey. Like any meaningful transformation, it requires constant introspection, courage, and adaptability. Life will present new challenges and opportunities, prompting you to reassess your values and recalibrate your goals. This continuous process of alignment ensures that your work remains a true reflection of who you are and what you stand for.

Practical steps can guide this journey:

- **Reflect Regularly**: Schedule moments of introspection. Ask yourself: "Does my work align with my values? Am I creating impact in ways that matter to me?"

- **Stay Open to Change**: Embrace the idea that purpose evolves. What fulfills you today may shift as you grow and encounter new experiences.

- **Celebrate Progress**: Recognize that even small steps toward a purpose-driven life are significant. Each effort contributes to the bigger picture of your legacy.

Building Your Legacy

Moving beyond the paycheck also means creating a legacy that transcends financial success. Legacy is about the ripple effect of your actions, the inspiration, ideas, and values you leave behind. It's what people remember about how you lived, not what you earned. Whether you mentor the next generation, champion a cause, or simply lead with integrity, your legacy becomes the ultimate measure of success.

As you embark on this journey, reflect on those who inspire you. Consider what they stood for and how they impacted others. These examples remind us that it's not the size of your bank account but the depth of your contributions that define a meaningful life.

Turning Work into Purpose

Work, at its best, is an expression of who we are. It's an opportunity to weave our passions, talents, and values into something greater than ourselves. By aligning your work with your purpose, you transform it from a means to an end into a fulfilling part of your life. The paycheck becomes a byproduct, not the sole reason, for what you do.

This shift requires courage, especially in a society that often equates success with wealth. But as countless individuals and organizations have demonstrated, pursuing purpose doesn't mean sacrificing financial security. In fact, aligning with purpose often leads to innovation, resilience, and even greater success, because it taps into intrinsic motivation and fosters deeper connections.

The Path Forward

The journey ahead is both exciting and transformative. Like a river carving its way through the landscape, your purpose will shape and be shaped by the experiences you encounter. This journey asks for your intentionality, your courage, and your commitment to living authentically.

You don't need to be Gandhi or Rockefeller to make a difference. Purpose is personal, it's found in the quiet acts of kindness, the commitment to growth, and the courage to align your life with your values. Whether you're mentoring a young professional, building a sustainable business, or simply showing up for your community, your efforts matter. The impact you make is what gives your work, and your life, its true value.

Beyond the Paycheck

As we part ways, remember that the paycheck is just the beginning. What lies beyond is a world of possibility, a life where meaning, connection, and contribution define your success. You hold the power to build a life that not only sustains you but also inspires and uplifts others. Turn your work into an expression of your values, and let your purpose illuminate the path ahead. This is your journey to create. Make it count.

Bonus Resources: Tools to Build Your Purpose Ecosystem

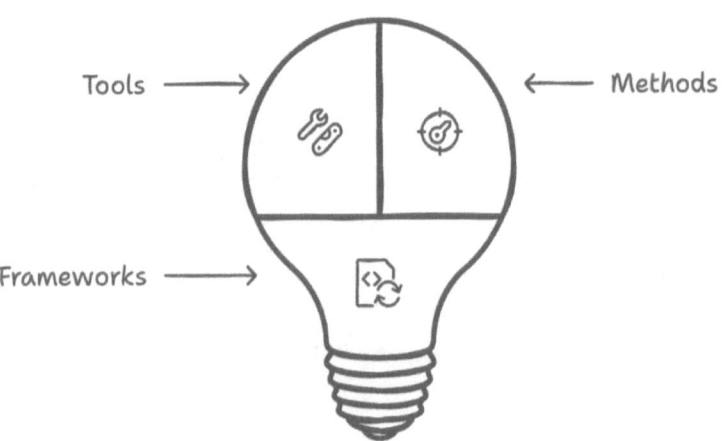

Building a life driven by purpose is not a passive process, it's an active, intentional practice requiring self-reflection, alignment with values, and consistent effort. To help you navigate this transformative journey, we present an in-depth guide to the tools, methods, and frameworks that can aid in discovering and living your purpose. These resources are designed to integrate seamlessly into your daily life, offering both structure and inspiration.

Purpose Discovery Worksheets

The Role of Purpose Discovery

Uncovering your "why" is the first step toward a life aligned with meaning and fulfillment. Purpose discovery worksheets are your structured guide to delving deep into your thoughts, experiences, and motivations.

Step-by-Step Worksheets

1. **The Five Whys Exercise**
    - Purpose: To uncover the deeper motivations behind your goals.
    - **How to Use**: Start with a goal or desire. Ask yourself "Why is this important?" five times in succession, digging deeper with each answer.
    - Example:
        o Goal: "I want to start a nonprofit."

- Why #1: "Because I want to help underprivileged youth."
- Why #2: "Because I've seen how lack of opportunities impacts their lives."
- Why #3: "Because I struggled with similar challenges growing up."
- Why #4: "Because empowering others gives me fulfillment."
- Why #5: "Because I want to create a legacy of positive change."

2. **Values Clarification**
    - Purpose: To identify the core principles guiding your decisions.
    - How to Use:
        - Write down ten values you believe define your actions (e.g., integrity, growth, creativity).
        - Rank them by importance.
        - Reflect on how these values show up in your daily life and where there may be misalignments.
    - **Example**: If "compassion" is a top value but is absent in your current work, this reveals a gap to address.

3. **Peak Moments Reflection**
    - Purpose: To identify what fulfillment feels like for you.

- **How to Use**: Reflect on three moments in your life when you felt truly alive and engaged. Write what made those moments meaningful.
- **Example**: "When I led a community art project, I felt creative, impactful, and connected to others."

Sample Purpose Discovery Worksheet

Step	Description	Example Entry
Step 1: The Five Whys	Write down a significant goal and ask 'Why is this important?' five times to uncover deeper motivations.	Goal: Start a nonprofit. Why 1: To make a difference. Why 2: To empower underprivileged youth. Why 3: To honor my own struggles growing up.
Step 2: Values Clarification	Create a list of your top 10 values and rank them by importance. Reflect on how aligned your actions are with these values.	Values: Integrity, Creativity, Empathy, Growth, Justice. Reflection: Current role aligns with Integrity and Creativity but lacks Empathy opportunities.
Step 3: Peak Moments Reflection	Think about three moments in your life when you felt fulfilled. Write down what made those moments meaningful.	Moment 1: Leading a community project - meaningful because it involved teamwork and impact.

Mind Mapping Templates

The Power of Mind Mapping

A mind map is a visual tool that helps organize thoughts, making it easier to identify patterns and connections between your strengths, values, and aspirations.

How to Create a Purpose Mind Map

1. **Central Theme**: Start with "My Purpose" in the center of your map.

2. **Branches**:

    - **Strengths**: Skills or talents where you naturally excel.

    - **Passions**: Activities that energize and excite you.

    - **Values**: Core beliefs that guide your decisions.

    - **Impact Areas**: Spheres where you want to make a difference (e.g., education, health, environment).

3. **Subcategories**: Expand each branch with specific details. For example, under "Strengths," add "problem-solving," "creativity," or "communication."

4. **Connections**: Look for overlapping themes between branches. This convergence often reveals your Zone of Genius.

Practical Example

Imagine someone who lists "teaching," "mentorship," and "education reform" as overlapping areas between passions and impact. This individual could explore careers or projects in education advocacy or curriculum development.

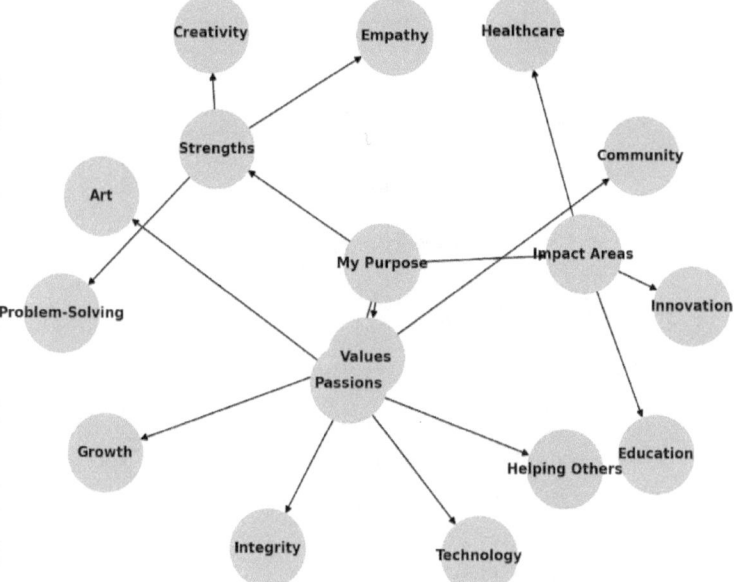

Sample Mind Map: Discovering My Purpose

The Intentionality Planner

Daily Practices for Purpose

Living intentionally means aligning your actions with your values every day. The Intentionality Planner helps you stay focused on this alignment.

Planner Features

1. **Morning Purpose Prompt**
    - Question: "What is one meaningful action I can take today?"

- Example: "Support a colleague with a challenging task."

2. **Top 3 Daily Priorities**
   - Focus on three actions that contribute to your goals.
   - Example:
     - Finish proposal for community project.
     - Reach out to mentor for advice.
     - Volunteer for local charity event.

3. **Midday Reflection**
   - Question: "Have I made progress toward my priorities?"
   - Example: "I completed the proposal draft and got valuable feedback from my mentor."

4. **Evening Reflection**
   - Questions:
     - "What went well today?"
     - "What could improve tomorrow?"
   - Example: "The charity event was fulfilling, but I need to manage time better during meetings."

Weekly Review

At the end of each week, assess your progress:

- What achievements are you proud of?
- What obstacles did you face, and how can you overcome them?

Sample Intentionality Planner

Section	Example Entries
Morning Purpose Prompt	What is one meaningful action I can take today? - 'Mentor a colleague'
Top 3 Daily Priorities	1. Prepare presentation on ethical business practices 2. Follow up on community project 3. Organize volunteer team
Midday Reflection	Have I made progress on my goals? - 'Yes, presentation is half complete.'
Evening Reflection	What went well today? - 'The mentoring session inspired great ideas.' What could improve? - 'Better time management for meetings.'

Recommended Reads and Resources

Books (non-sponsored, books that I have read personally and loved)

These books offer profound insights into purpose, habits, and personal development:

- *Atomic Habits* by James Clear: Practical strategies for building habits that align with your goals.
- *The Big Leap* by Gay Hendricks: Explore how to live in your Zone of Genius.
- *Start with Why* by Simon Sinek: Discover the power of understanding your "why."

- *Man's Search for Meaning* by Viktor Frankl: A philosophical exploration of purpose through the lens of Holocaust survival.
- *Grit* by Angela Duckworth: Insights into perseverance and passion.

Apps and Tools (non-Sponsored, apps that I have used personally and loved)

- **Headspace**: For mindfulness meditation to enhance self-awareness.
- **Trello**: Organize tasks visually, ideal for goal-setting.
- **Evernote**: A digital notebook for journaling and capturing reflections.

Purpose Ecosystem Framework

Building Your Ecosystem

- **Define Core Components**: Identify the values, strengths, and passions central to your purpose.
- **Align Environments**: Ensure your work and personal spaces reflect your purpose.
- **Create Feedback Loops**: Regularly review and refine your ecosystem based on new experiences.
- **Foster Collaboration**: Surround yourself with like-minded individuals who share your aspirations.

Case Study: A Purpose Ecosystem in Action

Consider an entrepreneur driven by sustainability. Their ecosystem includes:

- **Core Values**: Environmental stewardship, innovation.
- **Aligned Work**: A startup focusing on renewable energy.
- **Collaboration**: Partnerships with environmental NGOs.
- **Feedback Loop**: Regular customer surveys to align products with environmental impact goals.

Final Thoughts

The tools and frameworks shared in this book are not mere checkboxes to tick off, they are the architecture of a lifelong journey toward fulfillment and impact. Building your ecosystem of purpose is an ongoing process, one that demands curiosity, courage, and a willingness to evolve. It's about continuously reflecting on who you are, experimenting with what resonates, and aligning your daily choices with your deepest values. These resources are not static; they are dynamic, just like you. By integrating them into your life, you're not simply chasing career milestones or ticking off accomplishments. You are shaping a life of profound meaning, one where every step is intentional, every decision reflects your values, and every action contributes to the greater good.

This guide is yours to adapt, to personalize, and to make your own. Let it be the compass that points you toward your North Star, helping you navigate the complexities of life with clarity and confidence. As you embark on this journey, remember that purpose is not a final destination, it's a way of living. It's found in the small, deliberate moments of connection, in the courage to realign when life takes unexpected turns, and in the legacy, you leave behind through the lives you touch.

Today is the perfect day to start. Not tomorrow, not when the timing feels right, but now. Take these tools, step into your unique path, and begin crafting a life that not only fulfills you but inspires those around you. The world doesn't just need people who succeed, it needs people like you, who dare to live with intention and leave an enduring impact. Your journey starts here. Let it be one of purpose, passion, and profound transformation.

About the Author

Aakash is a relentless seeker of purpose. He believes in the power of intentionality and our ability to create lives of meaning and impact, together.

Described as "a dynamic thinker with a heart for transformation," Aakash has dedicated his professional journey to helping people unlock their full potential and reimagine success, not just as a destination, but as a fulfilling and purposeful journey. His vision? A world where individuals wake up inspired, navigate their days with clarity, and close them feeling deeply aligned with their values.

A passionate student of neuroscience and cognitive abilities, Aakash is fascinated by the science of human potential and the art of building purposeful lives. Over his career, he has mentored over 37,000 professionals, from ambitious entrepreneurs to dedicated 9-to-5 professionals, equipping them with the tools to lead with intention, find clarity in chaos, and thrive in uncertainty.

He is widely recognized for his contributions to the Talent Management space, earning accolades like Asia's Youngest Leader in Talent Space, Top 100 Emerging Leaders in India, and Top 30 Under 30 by WahStory (powered by SHRM). Whether collaborating with Fortune 500 organizations or pioneering change in fast-paced startups, Aakash's work is driven by a singular focus: to build systems and careers grounded in purpose and designed for impact.

What sets Aakash apart is his belief in blending science with humanity. His insights on purpose and leadership are shaped by his own experiences of navigating life's complexities, making his message not just aspirational, but relatable and actionable. He brings this unique perspective to his talks, mentoring sessions, and writing, inspiring audiences to think differently about success, fulfillment, and their own potential.

Aakash is not just a leader; he is a practitioner. His work embodies his belief that purpose isn't something you find, it's something you build, one intentional step at a time. Through his book, speaking engagements, and mentorship, he continues to help people realize that their greatest work is not what they earn, but the impact they leave behind.

Book Summary

The Empty Pay-check: Aligning Passion, Intent, and Success

Have you ever felt like your career is a treadmill, running fast but going nowhere? Have you achieved success only to feel an unsettling emptiness at the end of the day? **The Empty Pay-check** is here to change that.

This book is your call to stop chasing superficial achievements and start building a life driven by passion, fueled by intent, and rooted in purpose. It's not just about earning a paycheck, it's about earning fulfillment, creating impact, and leaving a legacy.

Through compelling stories, transformative tools, and insights from neuroscience and psychology, **The Empty Pay-check** helps you uncover your unique passion, align your career with your deepest values, and create a purpose-driven path to success. Whether you're feeling stuck, looking for a fresh start, or striving for greater meaning in your work, this book provides the practical steps and powerful inspiration you need.

Discover how to:

- Unearth your true passions and strengths.
- Build a career ecosystem that aligns with your purpose.
- Navigate transitions with clarity and courage.
- Lead with authenticity and intentionality.

Don't settle for a paycheck that feels empty. Step into a life of passion, impact, and success that resonates deeply with who you are. **The Empty Pay-check** isn't just a book, it's your blueprint for a meaningful career and a purpose-filled life.

Start your journey today.
The life you've been longing for is waiting.

www.ingramcontent.com/pod-product-compliance
Lightning Source LLC
LaVergne TN
LVHW041927070526
838199LV00051BA/2733